PUBLIC SPEAKING

Public Speaking Guide to Becoming a More Successful and Charismatic Leader

(Overcome Fear, Social Anxiety & Shyness to Influence Anyone)

Dale Noonan

Published by Rob Miles

© Dale Noonan

All Rights Reserved

Speaking: Public Speaking Guide to Becoming a More Successful and Charismatic Leader (Overcome Fear, Social Anxiety & Shyness to Influence Anyone)

ISBN 978-1-989990-19-3

All rights reserved. No part of this guide may be reproduced in any form without permission in writing from the publisher except in the case of brief quotations embodied in critical articles or reviews.

Legal & Disclaimer

The information contained in this book is not designed to replace or take the place of any form of medicine or professional medical advice. The information in this book has been provided for educational and entertainment purposes only.

The information contained in this book has been compiled from sources deemed reliable, and it is accurate to the best of the Author's knowledge; however, the Author cannot guarantee its accuracy and validity and cannot be held liable for any errors or omissions. Changes are periodically made to this book. You must consult your doctor or get professional medical advice before using any of the suggested remedies, techniques, or information in this book.

Upon using the information contained in this book, you agree to hold harmless the Author from and against any damages, costs, and expenses, including any legal fees potentially resulting from the application of any of the information provided by this guide. This disclaimer applies to any damages or injury caused by the use and application, whether directly or indirectly, of any advice or information presented, whether for breach of contract, tort, negligence, personal injury, criminal intent, or under any other cause of action.

You agree to accept all risks of using the information presented inside this book. You need to consult a professional medical practitioner in order to ensure you are both able and healthy enough to participate in this program.

Table of Contents

INTRODUCTION 1

CHAPTER 1: A BRIEF HISTORY 6

CHAPTER 2: THE THREE P'S 12

CHAPTER 3: STUDYING THE CRAFT 30

CHAPTER 4: REASONS WHY SOME PEOPLE FEAR PUBLIC SPEAKING 37

CHAPTER 5: THE TWO MOST IMPORTANT FACTORS 41

CHAPTER 6: STATUS 52

CHAPTER 7: UPHOLDING POSITIVE VIBES 65

CHAPTER 8: TRAITS OF GOOD PUBLIC SPEAKERS 72

CHAPTER 9: CONFIDENCE 77

CHAPTER 10: YOUR IMAGE 87

CHAPTER 11: HOW TO IMPROVE YOUR PUBLIC SPEAKING SKILLS 98

CHAPTER 13: CHANGE YOUR MINDSET ABOUT PUBLIC SPEAKING 106

CHAPTER 14: THE CLOSE 109

CHAPTER 15: THE WHAT 117

CHAPTER 16: PRACTICAL STEPS TO MANAGE PUBLIC SPEAKING FEAR 131

CHAPTER 17: PUBLIC SPEAKING IS EASY... IT'S ALL IN YOUR MIND! 138

CHAPTER 18: WRITING A MEMORABLE SPEECH 145

CHAPTER 19: ORGANIZING YOUR SPEECH 149

CHAPTER 20: GET SOME ROUTINE AND BANISH THE BUTTERFLIES 157

CHAPTER 21: LIST OF TOPICS 166

CHAPTER 22: THE BONUS SECTION 174

CHAPTER 23: DO YOU HAVE THE ABILITY TO DRAW PEOPLE AS A PROFESSIONAL SPEAKER? 181

CHAPTER 24: FACTORS THAT CAUSE PUBLIC SPEAKING ANXIOUSNESS 194

CHAPTER 25: HUMOR 197

CONCLUSION 204

Introduction

Have you ever sat through a presentation in which you felt detached from the speaker?

Perhaps it felt as if the speaker may as well have been delivering the presentation to an empty room, and that little purpose was served by you turning up to watch.

Maybe it appeared that they did not put any effort whatsoever into connecting with you as an audience, and as human beings.

Before we jump to conclusions, it is worth noting that this may not, in fact, have been the case. That is, the speaker may have put in more effort than it first appeared.

They may have been working their socks off to build an emotional connection with you and others who were present. They may simply not have been using the most effective techniques for doing so and not known how to go about improving in this regard.

It is also possible that the speaker was technically very skilled in some aspects of their communication. However, it may have been more of a priority for them, for example, to simply recite a particular piece of information, than to go one step further and convey that information in a way that really resonated with the audience after they left.

There may have been one or two particularly keen and attentive listeners who would have remembered a particular point or nugget of information however it was delivered. If it was a presentation about specific techniques for learning a new language, and this happened to be exactly what these keen listeners were hoping to hear from the get-go, it may not have made much difference in what way the speaker delivered the information.

However, the majority of the audience may not have been interested in this subject at all, in which case the information painstakingly delivered may not have found its target, all because of how it was conveyed.

The majority of people would be likely to switch off from the information being delivered, at least on an unconscious level. Unless, that is, the information was conveyed in such a way that engaged them, excited them, and made them feel valued as someone who has taken the time out of their busy schedule to learn something of value. In that case, even the most sceptical and closed-minded of attendees may have sat up and taken even a small amount of notice. Sometimes, that is all it takes.

Being an expert in a given topic does not necessarily mean you can successfully communicate that topic to a packed audience.

So, the next time you are preparing to deliver a presentation, give a motivational talk, or speak in front of an audience in any way, what are some techniques and principles you can apply to take it to the next level?

What can you do, specifically and practically, to break down the barriers between yourself and those looking up at you on your podium?

In this eBook, I will share six practical tips to help you to do just this, and in each case, give specific examples of how these can be used to achieve the desired effect.

I frequently do poetry readings in public, and am a committee member at a Toastmasters Club (Toastmasters International is a non-profit public speaking organization; to find a club near you, please visit. I have also dabbled in other types of public speaking, including stand-up comedy.

Whenever I am speaking in public, I make a point of putting each of these tips into practice in one way or another. I also make sure that I always listen to feedback on how effective they have been, and try to learn from this accordingly. Listening to feedback on a regular basis is one of the best ways to improve.

Throughout this eBook, I use the term 'speaker' fairly loosely. That is, by 'speaker', I am not just referring to those being paid to deliver a keynote, a lecture or any kind of formal speech. When this term is used throughout the book, it is intended to refer to anyone doing any form of public speaking in front of an audience.

The terms 'talk', 'presentation' and 'speech' are also used somewhat loosely and interchangeably.

My aim is to help you to become a better and more effective speaker by sharing what has worked for me and what I have seen work for others.

So, without further ado...

Chapter 1: A Brief History

Before we begin our exploration of public speaking, let us first take a trip down history to see how public speaking came about as we know it today.

Follow each step below to see how far we've gone from the earliest times. Use the information below to appreciate the changes that it underwent through the years. Also, use this timeline as an aid in deciding whether you want to be a part of and continue on the history of public speaking.

▪ About 2,500 years ago, it was part of the duties of young men in ancient Athens to deliver effective speeches

▪ During the time of Socrates, Plato and Artistotle, democracy was well on its way in Athens

▪ Citizens of the *polis* were called forth during the same time to testify in court and speak in legislative assemblies

- Debates on war, economics and politics are held by large Assemblies in Agora or the market place
- With the institution of the people's court by the ***Sage*** in 594-593 BCE, people could already take their complaints to the court and argue for their cases as well.
- People represented themselves and their families in court since there were no lawyers at that time
- Aristotle identified ***ethos, logos*** and ***pathos*** (or credibility, logic and emotional appeals) as intrinsic components of a good speech
- After Rome succeeded over Athens, Marcus Cicero rose to power as a lawyer, orator, politician and philosopher. He pioneered the 5 canons of rhetoric that are still used today which are invention, arrangement, style, memory and delivery

After reading some of the pivotal events in the history of public speaking, how do you think these circumstances shape our public speaking today?

It's More Than Just Talk

Words are the nanobots of life. They may be very small but they can make a considerable amount of impact. Certainly, at one point in your life, you have craved for soothing words to comfort your soul. It could be after a great loss, defeat or a break up – but you just knew that hearing some kind and comforting words can save your day. Likewise, letting lose words that were born out of anger and resentment can not only ruin one's day but also has the power to ruin a life and a relationship. Words are impactful that way. That is why choosing, using and expressing them correctly for whatever purpose needed can be beneficial to all parties involved. Business and personal relationships can thrive with good and effective communication.

Finding the importance of good communication and public speaking skills is easy. Since it is connected to various aspects of our lives one way or another, its fruits will undoubtedly abound. You wouldn't have to start playing a guessing game when trying to find out what's in it for you if ever you decide to enhance your public speaking skills. Here are some of the rewards you should expect when you decide to do so.

☐Preparing becomes a habit: speaking in front of a lot of people is not an easy task. Though others may be fortunate enough to be given a topic to talk about, it's not always the case. It may also happen that a speaker may be given the freedom to choose the topic and what to go into specifically. This doubles the task as well as the challenge faced by speakers. With that, adequate preparation becomes necessary. Repeating best practices when preparing for a speech helps turn them into good habits that can be applied in other tasks as well.

☐Enhanced self confidence: A number of surveys and researches showed that most people would choose death over having to speak in front of an audience. Though this may sound outrageous, this truth haunts millions of people around the globe. However, those who were able to overcome ***glossophobia*** or fear of public speaking really have it better. Being able to speak in front of a large audience is a victory that can easily eliminate small challenges. People who are able to conduct themselves appropriately in front of a crowd generally experience fewer difficulties in networking, job interviews, dealing with difficult people and other interpersonal relationships.

☐Increased opportunities: Being articulate is one of the best ways to get noticed and be held above the rest. People who exude high confidence levels are often given more chances to shine mainly because they look the part and they demonstrate that they are capable in doing so. Also, being able to send right messages across effectively can win you friends and contracts among others that could be of great help to increase your credibility.

Now that you've seen how having good public speaking skills can benefit many, if not all, aspects of your life – are you ready take that first step to a better life?

Chapter 2: The Three P's

- Introduction
- The secret for presentation success
- Getting the preparation balance right
- Understanding your audience's needs
- What do people expect from the presentation
- What do they want from the presentation
- What can you deliver?
- The crucial questions you must ask to meet an audience needs
  - What do they want?
  - What do they know?
- Are there any questions?
  - Will there be questions?
  - Can I answer them?
- Dealing with questions
  - How to effectively answer questions from the floor
- Understanding your audience
  - What is the audience dynamic
- Scripting Techniques

- What you need is not a script...
- **Creating Cue Cards**
- Use of cue cards
- Level of content required
- **Rehearsing**
- How to rehearse

Introduction

In this section we are going to introduce the Three Ps. They are:

- Preparation
- Preparation
- Preparation

This will seem obvious; however, a lack of effective preparation will be the downfall of any presentation. The key word is effective preparation. This is ensuring that not only have you prepared a set of slides, but that you are aware of the audience, the environment and your message. Once all of these elements are in place you will have been well on the way to winning over the audience before you have even stood up to speak!

In this section we will take you through the methods you should employ when preparing for a presentation.

Getting the preparation balance right

On the last we introduced the Three Ps and I told you of the importance of preparation; however, there is a caveat. You do need to get the balance right for your preparation. You may not believe it, but you can be too prepared for a presentation with the result that you come across as stilted or over-rehearsed.

You should ensure that you have taken your preparation steps and that you have rehearsed your presentation, however you should resist the temptation to be so prepared that you know your content and your presentation so well that you seem to be reciting content from memory with no concern for the audience.

You are looking for a stage where you are comfortable with the content and the presentation, you know how you will present and you are aware of the aims and objectives and the points you wish to make. This is the stage to stop. Take a break, you are ready to go!

By all means keep the ideas fresh in your mind, but don't keep going over the presentation again and again; you need it to be fresh for your audience. The impression you want to give is that this is the first time you have shared your presentation with anyone (even if you have given the presentation many times before).

Understanding your audience's needs

The first step in the preparation for any presentation is an understanding of what the audience wants to get out of it. It is important to note that this may not be what the title of the presentation you have been given is. You need to ensure that you know as much as you can about your audience before you stand before them.

So, for example:
- Who are the audience?

o What is their level of experience and knowledge?

o It is vital to ensure that you do not stand up and tell them what they already knew or bamboozle them with content which is too complex.

o What is the dynamic? – Are the audience going to be senior directors or shop-floor staff? You need to consider your content and language to meet the needs of the audience. o Where have they come from?

o Is this a single company or team or is this a public forum? If they do come from one organisation you can make sure that you use some of their house language (the internal terms and phrases each organisation uses) to show affinity with them.

- What do they expect from the presentation?

o Do their aims and objectives match the ones you have set for your presentation?

o What is their expectation for the presentation? Are they expecting a staid and boring speech, is this what you should deliver?

- What do they want from the presentation?

o Do they have specific items of information which are key to them and which they simply must know about? So many presentations I have seen presenters giving reams of information which people gloss over when all they wanted was a short explanation.

- What can you deliver?

o This is the final vital point. Are there items which the audience would like to have but you just cannot deliver? Perhaps something has not been decided upon or finalised

o It is important, where you can, to not just ignore these items. Be honest if you cannot talk about something; at least tell the audience this and the reason why. Tell them when they will get this information.

The crucial questions you must ask to meet an audience's needs The previous set of questions allowed us to discover who the audience were and what they expected and wanted from the presentation, however there are two other major areas you need to review. Firstly, what does the audience already know?

There is no point in boring your audience by telling them information they already know, however you would be amazed how many times presenters do not ask this simple question. In fact by asking who the audience is you should have a much better idea of their knowledge level.

Of course, this is sometimes not as simple as yes, they have knowledge of some area or no, they do not. You may find that you have a mixed audience or, worst still, people who turn up at the last minute knowing nothing about what you are talking about!

So how can you cope? Try this three-step plan: 1. Know the audience – Find out who the audience will be, then ask the organiser or even some audience members what they know already.

2. Be prepared – Just in case, it is worth the effort to have a couple of 'background slides' which quickly cover the background to what you are presenting. You can quickly introduce these as a set of 'as you know already' facts or go into more detail if required.

3. Read the audience – Watch the body language. Are they bored or disinterested? Is it time to move on!

Are there any questions?

Are you ready to answer questions about your presentation? There are three things you need to consider:

● do you feel ready to give an authoritative answer to a question which may come up? – Did you need to get permission or authority to detail any of the content within your presentation? Do you have the knowledge and permission to answer the sort of questions which may come up?

- is it the right forum to ask for questions? – You need to consider if it will be logistically possible for questions to be handled. For example, a large auditorium may require a number of people with radio microphones to ensure a question is audible to the audience. Is this in place? Equally, what is the expectation for the event - if you ask for questions from the floor will every speaker be expected to do the same?
- will there be any questions? – There can be a horrible silence which follows a call for questions and none of the audience want to say anything (known in the trade as a 'tumbleweed moment'!). The response to this is to be confident and state that you must have covered the content well.

Asking questions can be a simple and useful way to involve the audience and create a more interactive presentation. If you have answered the questions above, you should be ready for questions. The next step is being able to deal with them effectively.

Dealing with questions

Effectively dealing with questions can provide an excellent element for a presentation, however there are a few hints and tips which will allow you to ensure your Q&A sessions go smoothly:

- use a roving microphone – In all but the smallest rooms you will find that it is useful to employ a person (or people) with a roving microphone. This will allow the entire audience to clearly hear the question from the delegate.
- but - use the roving microphone effectively – Be aware that you need to ensure that your microphone wrangler keeps some control over the microphone. It is preferable that the mic is controlled by a sound engineer (who will fade up the mic when the delegate asks a question). If this is not possible ensure that they switch the mic on before handing it to the delegate. It can be embarrassing if the mic

does not work and can affect your 'Alpha Presenter' position.

• beware 'mic grab' – mic grab is when a delegate takes the microphone and will not hand it back, determined to ask more questions or worst still to try to argue with you as the presenter. We will deal with difficult people later in the ebook, however the best policy is for the mic wrangler to take back the microphone when the question has been completed or to hold the microphone for the delegate. Everyone with a question should be given their chance to speak so it is important to firmly, yet politely, ensure that individuals do not take over.

• repeat the question – repeating the question confirms that you have understood what the delegate is asking and ensures that the entire audience has also clearly understood. The delegate may not have spoken clearly and even though you may have heard you must stop the questions becoming a one to one conversation.

- you should have factored time into your presentation for questions; do not allow the session to overrun. At the required time thank the audience and offer to take any further questions 'off-line' after the presentation.

Understanding your audience

We know who your audience is, we know what they want, however there is one more thing which you should be aware of and that is the audience dynamic.

The audience dynamic refers to your audience's mood and body language during your presentation. It is important to watch for changes in the audience as you speak. You will be looking for signs that they are bored or irritated:

- are they becoming bored? – yawning, shuffling papers or reading something else, basically not paying attention to you or the presentation

- are they becoming irritated? – crossed arms, whispering or talking between delegates, people walking out.

The signs will usually start subtly and then increase. The challenge is to do something about the changing dynamic when you first see it. If it is boredom, is this something to do with you? (Ouch – but we have to consider it!) Try picking up the pace; perhaps try asking a question of the audience with a show of hands or similar to get them interacting.

If it is irritation, and this is generally rare, you need to weigh up what may be causing the issue. Were there any items you were aware of in your preparation which may cause an issue with the audience? Again you may do well to move on in your content or, if the issue is not going away, to close the presentation early.

Generally good preparation will prevent these issues, however you are ready if you have an unexpected issue.

Scripting Techniques

Unless you really know your subject inside out, you will need to prepare some form of script for your presentation. Scripts:

- ensure you cover all of the content you intend to within a presentation
- give you structure and a running order for the points you are going to cover
- act as an aid to your memory while you present.

The only thing a script is not; is a script! Okay, that is a weird statement, however when you present you should be spending your time interacting with the audience; you cannot do this and read a script. The audience will soon guess you are reading the content word for word and will often wonder why you didn't just send the copy to them and save the time of attending the presentation!

You need to know enough of your content and your presentation to be able to have a few words which you can say about each slide somewhat 'off the cuff'. You have two ways to remember what to say: the content of your slides and your cue cards.

Creating Cue Cards

Previously I told you that you should not have a script; what you need to develop is a set of simple cue cards which cover the main points you want to cover on each slide:

The cue cards should be quite small (A5 index card or less) with clear text. The contents should not be a full script for the slide, but bullet points or facts which you wish to ensure that you cover at this point in the presentation.

Write the cards out clearly (or print using a nice large font you can glance at quickly) and then punch a hole in the top left hand corner and attach them together with a treasury tag. Attaching them together is important – just think what would happen if you dropped them and got them out of order!

You should then place them in front of you (or hold them in your hand) and practice glancing at the contents. This, with the pictures or text on the slide, should be all you need.

Rehearsing

A good rehearsal can be a great way to ensure that you are comfortable with your presentation and script. There are two main types of rehearsal: mirror and in-situ.

Mirror Rehearsals

They are called mirror rehearsals for the simple reason that you should find a mirror (full length is best) and practice giving your presentation. You should ensure that you are comfortable with the content (cut and change as required – it is easier here than on stage!) and also that you are interacting with the audience.

Make sure that you are looking up and keeping eye contact with the audience (you, in this case). You should ensure you are not just reading your cue cards. If you are, you need to ensure that you practise using them until they are second nature.

Note – you can replace the mirror with a video camera if you wish, however this can lack the instant feedback you get from looking yourself in the eyes.

In-situ Rehearsals

This is the ultimate luxury, but one you should try to afford yourself. This is to get to the venue early and have a chance to practice on stage with the live presentation.

Mirror rehearsals are great for practice at home before the event; you should ensure you are happy with the content and that you know what you will be speaking about. In-situ rehearsals give you an opportunity to ensure you are comfortable with the venue and equipment. Where will I be standing, how do I move on slides, where do I walk on and off the stage?

Combining the two types of rehearsal will ensure you have both the presentation content and the technology under your control and you will be ready to knock 'em dead!

Section Review

In this section we have started to build our effective presentation. We have:

- learnt the value of preparation, without preparing too much!
- found out about the needs of our audience: who they are and what they want to hear
- asked the crucial questions about the presentation: we know the audience, we are prepared and we read the body language for any issues
- learnt when to ask for questions and how to deal with them
- understood the difference between a script and cue cards
- understood how to rehearse.

Now we will build on these tools to become a perfect presenter!

Chapter 3: Studying The Craft

- You're in a very unique position today. More than ever before, you have the opportunity to become a better speaker by learning from the greats, because you live in the age of the internet. 50 years ago, your only options were observation, a good friend or a mentor to advise you, or maybe a Dale Carnegie Training Course. 20 years ago, you still had to shell out a lot of money for VHS-, or eventually, DVD-based training. Not today. In the age of the internet, you only need your favorite search engine, and there are few limits to what you can find.

The very best speakers from politics, business, sports, and entertainment are right there at your fingertips. Spend time watching them. At first, don't take notes. Just watch and think about what they're doing. Now after watching at least a couple hour's worth of video, stop and step away for a day or two. When you come back after letting all of that material marinate in your brain, you'll feel more ready and able to start picking apart what they're actually doing as speakers.

And get ready to take some notes. I want you to watch your favorite video clips again. This time, think carefully about each of these variables: the use of hands to complement what's being said, the movement of the head, the use of eye contact, facial expressions, voice volume and changes in volume, vocal pace, and the use of pauses. There are many variables, but these are the most important general issues to think about as you get started.

I want you to know that with increased familiarity will come increased comfort as a speaker. Keep these factors in mind, and take notes about what you're watching on the video. You'll notice that my list of variables didn't include the message, the content of what they're saying. To be a great speaker, you do need solid content.

But here, we're talking about the basic mechanics of speaking. And here's what we know about speeches. Half or more of the value others perceive in your speech comes not from the words you use, but from the delivery, which really is the list of variables I mentioned a moment ago.

Here's another fact you really need to remember. Nobody starts out as a great speaker, nobody. Here's one of my favorite quotes. This is from Ralph Waldo Emerson, who once said, "All great speakers were bad speakers at first." I'll go even further. All speakers experience nerves. I'm not kidding, that goes for me too. I'm a professional speaker. I give speeches at corporate events for a living, and I get nervous before every single event. You can learn to do what I did, which is to control the nerves and use them to help you deliver with energy instead of allowing them to cause you problems.

It all starts with watching the greats, analyzing them using the variables we covered, and then slowly improving what you're doing as a speaker, variable by variable. With patience and a little time, you just might become a great speaker too.

Finding opportunities to speak

- I have some bad news, and some good news. The bad news is that if you want to overcome the fear of public speaking, you'll have to speak a lot. The good news is that the more you speak, the more you'll learn to calm yourself, and feel pretty comfortable while speaking. I want you to actively look for opportunities to speak. You can even create opportunities. There are many available to you at work and outside of work. I'm going to mention several you might consider, but first, let's be clear about what you're trying to do.

You're collecting data, data about yourself, data on each of the major variables of your speech delivery, which we've mentioned before; the use of hands to compliment what's being said, the movement of the head, the use of eye contact, facial expressions, voice volume and changes in volume, vocal pace, and the use of pauses. You're going to gather data a few different ways. Self-reflection, that is your own analysis of how you did. Audience reactions, for example, are they sleeping or sitting on the edge of their seat? Feedback you solicit, here I suggest you start simple with a few personal conversations.

And last, but certainly not least, video of you speaking. Nothing is as blunt and useful as video because video doesn't lie. I want to encourage you to watch that video and think about the other forms of feedback too, all while thinking through the variables we just mentioned a moment ago. To start, choose one variable, whichever one is your biggest area for improvement, and work on that the next time you speak. Which leads us to thinking about opportunities to speak.

At work you have department meetings, briefings to superiors, pitches made to clients, brown-bag lunches, affinity group meetings, and many types of training environments. Don't wait to be told to speak, ask for the opportunity. You might run a meeting, facilitate a brown-bag talk, or share your expertise in a training environment. Outside of work there are many additional opportunities. For example, speaking at church, as a part of a study group or support group. Speaking at meetings for civic or social groups, for example Rotary clubs, the Kiwanis club and so on.

Or, speaking as an expert at schools in the community. Or maybe one of the many local business associations. And don't forget to look into the Toastmasters, the oldest and most successful group for people who wish to become better speakers. Once you start actually looking, you might be surprised how many readily available opportunities to speak there are all around you. I want you to remember, this is a process of collecting data one variable at a time. The question is not 'Can you become a better speaker?'.

The only question is 'Will you become a better speaker?'. Start looking now for opportunities to collect the needed data.

Chapter 4: Reasons Why Some People Fear Public Speaking

The second chapter has made it clear that public speaking is both important and beneficial. It is important because certain events and situations in our life will someday call for it, and it is beneficial because it gives us an edge from other people. Despite the many reasons why public speaking is important, why are some people afraid of speaking in public? This chapter will inform you some of the reasons why some people fear public speaking.

Being afraid to speak in public is normal; this is a fear called glossophobia. One of the most common reasons why people fear public speaking is because they are afraid to commit mistakes. As mentioned earlier, public speaking can boost self-confidence. However, if the was not delivered properly, it can be a problem. Improper delivery of public speech will produce unintended results that can affect the quality of your speech, as well as your credibility as a speaker.

Because of the improvements made by technology, there are new ways for people to communicate. An example of this is through the Internet and social media. Because of this, many people become so used to talking to people only through this medium. They find it difficult to talk to a large number of people because they are more comfortable communicating with them online. Some people have fear of public speaking, primarily because they were not exposed to it.

Glossophobia can also arise from self-consciousness. When there are many people watching you, you begin to become conscious of how you look on stage, how you talk, what the sound of your voice is, and other factors. You begin wondering about what they think of you and how they judge your speech. Because of self-consciousness, you sometimes develop negative thoughts such as the amount of mistakes that you may commit, or the audience laughing at your mistakes, and many more. Once these things come into your mind, you become afraid and nervous.

Fear of public speaking can also be due to past failures. Perhaps you someone asked you to speak in public before, but you failed to deliver it properly. You may have committed numerous mistakes, or may have received negative judgments from the audience. You associate public speaking with the bad things that has happened to you before. Because of this, you become afraid that those events will happen again.

When engaged in a public speaking activity, you feel greater fear when you are not well prepared with your speech. Perhaps you do not have enough time to research and outline your speech, or you forgot some materials that are necessary in delivering it. Lack of preparation can be one reason why you are afraid to deliver a speech in public.

Mentioned above are just some of the many possible causes of fear in public speaking. Speakers encounter fear in public speaker because even before they have delivered the speech, they are already thinking of negative thoughts. They focus too much on what the audience may say about them, rather than focusing on their topics and the structure of their speeches.

What are the things that a speaker needs to do whenever he or she is faced with these things? What are the measures that he or she needs to take before delivering his or her speech in order for him or her to lessen his or her fear and nervousness? The next chapter will give you some tips on the things that you need to do before you deliver your speech.

Chapter 5: The Two Most Important Factors

The story of Jesus turning five loaves of bread and two fishes to feed five thousand people was amazing. At the initial, all what the disciples saw with the present situation was an impossible feat; all what they saw with the provision of the young lad was an impossible situation.

While they were very good in the principles of accounting, and by trying hard to let Jesus see how much it would and would not cost to feed such great multitudes of people, all that Jesus saw and needed was just five loaves and two small fishes from a **young lad who knew what little meant when it falls into the hand of the Great Master.**

Using What Is Inconsequential to Generate Massive Success

Surprisingly, what was looked down upon as inconsequential was the very provision used to feed thousands of multitudes. So the question is asked: what is that thing in your own life or in your possession that you've been looking down on?

Maybe like the little lad, the only thing you have left in your possession are five miserable loaves of bread and two small fishes. Did you get that? **Five loaves of bread and two SMALL fishes!**
And hey, don't miss that **SMALL** part in that story. S-M-A-L-L! Did you get that? And maybe that is the reason why you're affirming in the lie that with it you can't pay off your bill, that you can't set off your debt, and that you can't put food on your table.
Whatever the reason and whatever it is – five . . . two . . . small . . . little . . . inconsequential or call it what you may - if only you could turn it over to the Man who cannot be limited or intimidated with your five, two, small, little, or inconsequential possessions, and who is not and cannot be constrained with the laws of gravity,

science, technology or accounting principles, you will be surprised to what extent it would take you and what, in the long run, you would achieve with it – financially speaking!

Back then there was nothing like food science and technology, I guess. Or even if there were, it was not as advanced and sophisticated as the one the modern World now boasts of. But that day the law of science and accounting proved inconsequential! They became totally useless!

You remember the story of Moses and the Rod? Yeah, that too beats the law of science and technology. **"And the Lord said unto him, What is that in thine hand? And he said, *A rod"* (Exodus 4:2, Emphasis Added).**

Maybe that's all you need – a rod; or maybe that's all you have – a rod. Interestingly, that's all that is needed to part the Red Sea in your speaking engagement.

You see, Moses almost subjected himself into a life of perpetual fear and slavery because of his lack of faith in the God who had called him out of Egypt in order to lead the children of Israel into the Promised Land.

In fact God had to push him hard enough to see the potential of what he had - a rod, regardless of how totally meaningless it seems to change and better his life and that of the children of Israel, and taught him how to harness it!

The Two Factors to Getting Results

Now, like the story of the five loaves of bread and two small fishes that was used to feed five thousand people, and the Rod of Moses which was used to perform great signs and wonders, the two most important factors to consider before building a successful speaking business, and if you can remember these two most important factors are . . .

1. What you know, have, or love talking about which could be the five loaves of bread, two small fishes or a rod.
2. Your target audience.

These are very vital to every aspect if you must build and/or host a successful speaking event. Why? Because they will help you to . . .

1 Build and develop your script in line with what you know, have, or love talking about with your target audience in mind.

2 Create a sense of fulfillment talking about what you know or what excites you and earning from it.

3 Ability to answer questions related to what you're knowledgeable about

Remember, the best way to really earn from your speaking business is to . . .

Give a speech related to what you KNOW, HAVE OR LOVE TALKING ABOUT!

Be passionate about what you know or have (i.e. your gift) and be willing to carry out research in line with that area.

Many who want to be successful in their speaking business, who wants to turn words into money are today not successful, not because they don't have what it takes but because they have failed to make and to be committed to research which is paramount to their topic.

At such, they say the same thing over and over again as their style of delivery becomes stale, and very, very, very bad!

They go into speaking business as if they are into it for themselves! They don't know how to use humor, personal story and experience to reach and connect with their audience.

The principle to success in life is generally the same everywhere you go. And you can only succeed in your speaking business if you can make adequate preparation before you set off, knowing your subject in and out, fashioning what you know to the benefit of your audience and consequently, knowing your audience before hand and so on.

What to Know If You Must Start Successfully

Here are few important keynotes of what you should know before venturing into the business proper . . .

1 Your look and your appearance - A good look or appearance gender assurance and believability. It makes you possess that "god-like appearance", or as someone who really knows his (or her) subject from start to finish.

Sometimes, however, your looks and appearance are predicated on the caliber of people that will be gracing your speaking event, or that you're called to talk to. So try to look at your best!

Remember the story of the prodigal son who came back home, and how he was adorned with the finest apparel from his head to his toes? The Bible reads, **"But the father said to his servants, Bring forth the best robe, and put it on him; and put a ring on his hand, and shoes on his feet"** (Luke 15:22).

However, you shouldn't over do it. Speaking business is not a fashion parade! It's not about an angel walking on an aisle. But you must look at your best!

2 *The tone of your speech* – Your speech must be inspiring, motivating, challenging and MUST have the power to create that sense of fulfillment, always!

Furthermore, you must be practical rather than giving hypes and gimmicks, and stop playing around the bush instead of going after the bush. Your audience should be able to connect to your idea or opinion when you speak.

Do you remember when God gathered the children of Israel to talk to them at Mount Sinai after they came out of Egypt?

Whew! It was terrible! They couldn't withstand the thunderous voice! In fact it scared the spleen out of them that they had to push Moses to listen to God on their behalf! You don't want to sound like a booing machine, or would you?

3 The length of your speech - If you want to get the best from your speaking business by just organizing and giving speech on what you know, have, or love doing or talking about, you must **be conscious of your time frame.** If you over do it, rather than inspire and challenge your audience you will weary and bore them to death!

Hence you must be able to condense your speech in such a way that both you and your audience will fill motivated and fulfilled. At least none of you should have that feeling that either of you is wasting each other's time, or trying to lord it over one another.

As a result you will need to develop the ability to **recognize and interpret body language.** The bottom-line, however, is this . . .

4 **Know your audience** - What are their expectations? What do they (or you) think might hinder them from getting the best

from your speaking engagement? If you know your audience it would be easy to relate with them on their terms.

Although the word, **"Know your audience"** is easier said than done; because this is very difficult especially when you realize that your audience are made of different personalities from different home, background, training and had different perspectives to life.

Why? Because you can't reach, connect and know everyone on their terms! So it is easy for you to design your thoughts and ideas from your own perspective than from the perspective of your audience.

Thus, don't make the mistake of hosting your speaking event simply to meet your own needs and satisfy your ego. You must learn to see beyond that and learn to see from the eyes of your audience.

Hence, you must always remember the word: **know your audience!** It is one of the most vital key to your success as a speaker. And you must never forget that.

Chapter 6: Status

What We Mean By 'Status'

The word *Status* can mean a number of things. Today, social networking sites spring to mind, and we think of our current 'state of mind' or of what our situation is at this given moment.

However another definition of *Status* (the one that interests us), is the *state of a person in comparison with others*. This has nothing to do with actual superiority, or thinking you're superior in comparison to other people, but rather an awareness of the scale from Low Status to High Status, and where you fit into it.

As performers we use the status scale when thinking about characters, so if playing a Low Status character (a beggar, a thief, etc.) we will adopt the mannerisms and speech patterns relevant to the character's status. When speaking in public or in front of an audience, you want to aim for High Status qualities, and this section contains exercises and tips on how to achieve that, without appearing arrogant and without 'putting on a character'.

The 'C' Word

When I ask people "what is the most important quality for a public speaker to have?" everyone has the same answer: Confidence.

Confidence is the quality in a person that makes you subconsciously think "they know what they're talking about, I can trust them". That's what every public speaker aims for, because simply put, confidence makes people listen to you, and if *you* have confidence, people will have confidence *in you*, and in what you're telling them.

But here's an actor's secret that you might not be expecting to hear: it really doesn't matter *at all* if you actually feel confident or not. What matters is that you can have the *appearance* of confidence. Some people naturally have confidence, some people don't, it's the same with actors as it is with everyone else - but everyone gets stage-fright and at points suffer from a 'lack of confidence', it's just that some people know how to hide it better than others.

Hopefully some of the exercises and tips in this guide will help you to be more confident when speaking in public, but they're mainly designed to deal with the technical details of making sure people can hear you correctly and that you present yourself professionally. Personal confidence is a different thing altogether, only you can teach yourself to be more confident as a person. But these exercises can give you the tools to remain calm, to produce a strong and authoritative voice, to help remember your train of thought, and how to stand professionally, but becoming more confident as a person takes one thing: practice.

What you'll find here are tricks to give you an appearance of confidence, whether you have it or not, and by practicing them you can prepare yourself to speak better. Then each time you speak you will hopefully learn more about what you should and shouldn't do, and your confidence will slowly build up.

The following exercises will give you ways to physically give yourself a High Status quality, and more importantly, that look of confidence.

1. Sternum Lift

Your sternum, or breastbone, is located in the middle of your chest, and connects your upper ribs to one another. To give yourself an instant appearance of confidence and high status, all you have to do is lift this area up. It sounds easy, but there's a trick to doing it right, and it takes practice, and a lot of looking in the mirror to make sure you aren't over-doing it (which can translate as cockiness, or look like you're 'advertising your assets').

The first method of doing this is what a lot of classical actors do before they go on stage to perform:

Stand up with a straight back and your arms by your sides.

As you breathe in, simultaneously raise your arms up above your head, and rise onto your tiptoes, lifting up in your chest as you reach for the ceiling.

Breathe out and lower your arms, bringing yourself back from tiptoes, but keep your chest in exactly the same position as it was when your arms were in the air.

Walk around holding your sternum up, and feel the effect it has on your walking pattern. Look in a mirror and adjust the position if you think you're over-doing it, but try to remember what it feels like and you might find the same method useful before you have to speak.

2. Zipping Up

The second method of lifting your sternum is a little less dramatic, but can still give you a look of confidence and high status.

Simply pretend you're zipping up a really tight jacket. Use your hands to hold an imaginary zip in place.

Pull the imaginary zip up with your right hand, and as you do so, lift up the front of your chest, and push down with your back. As with the first Sternum Lift, walk around and find the best position for you.

3. Quads

One of the qualities of confidence is having the right energy. If you appear to have low energy you could be seen as boring or tired, but on the other hand if you show too high energy you might appear over excited or just like you've had too much coffee. A good speaker should aim for a bright, springy quality, both physically and vocally. One way to achieve a springy physicality is to work from the ground up, and this exercise does just that:

Standing with your back straight, either barefoot, in socks, or loose comfortable shoes, raise onto your tiptoes and hold.

Quickly lower yourself and as your heels are just about to touch the ground, raise back up onto tiptoes. Keep the motion going and do 50 quick repetitions, until you can feel the stretch in your quadriceps.

You'd be amazed just how much this can help your physicality. It gives you a stronger connection to the ground and is great if your speech involves walking to and from a certain area to address your audience. Your first and last impressions are very important after all, and it often begins with your approach to the podium!

4. Less Is More

One of the things that will drop your status is unnecessary movement. Learning how to eliminate unwanted mannerisms is a must for gaining a high status, and it begins by realising what these mannerisms are. This exercise will increase your awareness of distracting mannerisms, so that you can avoid them when you're speaking. You'll need a line or two of speech, it doesn't have to be something serious, just something you can use to pretend you're in a speaking or presentation situation. Pick an object or two in the room that can be your audience, and deliver the lines to them:

Say your lines with your hands in your pockets - this is an all too common error that makes a speaker look less confident.

Say your lines while rocking or swaying gently from side to side - most people who do this don't even realise they're doing it, but it communicates to an audience that you don't feel comfortable, it's you body's way of saying "get me out of here!", but it can be repressed if you become aware you're doing it.

Repeat your lines while tapping your fingers on your legs, arms or paper, and biting your lip occasionally - another two common signals that might seem nothing to you while you're doing them, but hint to your listeners that you lack confidence.

Repeat your lines while playing with your hair or hands - we've all seen and done this from time to time. Subconscious hair and hand fiddling can actually really annoy some listeners, and it's a common actors issue too. If you're thinking "I don't know what to do with my hands though!", as many actors do, the following *gesture* exercises and tips might help.

Gesturing

Gesturing is the use of your body (usually hands), to reinforce and physically punctuate your vocal message. You can use gesturing to effectively convey your thoughts and feelings physically to the audience, but it has to be done clearly, and in moderation.

Clear gesturing precisely follows your vocal message, and is used as physical punctuation: for example if you're proposing a theory or a rhetorical question, you might make one, clear and pointed open hand gesture with one hand, then as you move on, bring your hand back fluidly.

Your hands should never look dead by your sides, but when not gesturing should be held in a neutral, and natural position in front of you or loosely with bent elbows. If you're holding papers, try and hold them in one hand, and gesture with your other.

Moderation is important because some people assume they should be gesturing all the time, and punctuate every word. This can often give the impression that the speaker is overexcited and has a lot of nervous energy, or is trying to waft away flies. Gestures should be rationed for precise points, should be practiced beforehand, and should be clear and fluid.

5. Open Hands

A good gesture for communicating openness and comfortability, is the aptly named Open Hands.

All you need to do is hold out your hands in front of you, with your palms facing up, as you speak (see photo below). Spread out your fingers in an open, welcoming way, but move slowly so your listeners aren't taken aback - remember, you're trying to put them at ease and make them watch and listen to you.

This gesture is great for opening a speech, and can also be done with one hand instead of two. It may seem simple but that's the key to its success, this gesture can subliminally put an audience at ease and give your speech a structure.

6. The Point Maker

A simple gesture to use when you're making a specific point or trying to draw attention to a certain section of your speech is The Point Maker. This has a number of forms, but the simplest and least intrusive are pictured below:

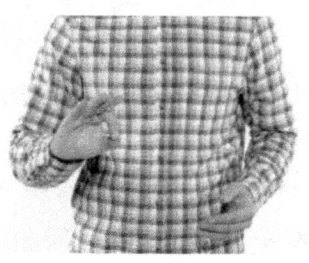

Notice how in both the hands are turned downwards. Turning your hands over is an indication of change in tone or importance, and these gestures work when you fluidly move from open, upward facing palms, to The Point Maker, as you deliver an important line.

Chapter 7: Upholding Positive Vibes

You are what you think. In the public speaking world, there are two kinds of speakers. First is the one who is confident, smart-looking, and prepared to stand in front, and thinks that people will applaud and praise him for a speech well done, while the other one is clouded with gloomy thoughts that he or she might not successfully make it through.

Of course, you want to be the first one, right? Who would not want a successful presentation?

Speaking in front a huge crowd may really be nerving to most people, that they even come to a point wherein they fear it. Believing that everything will slip out from your fingers and get out of control, that your mind will be blocked and you will stutter your practiced delivery, and that your audience will not listen or understand. You would just make the entire situation worse and you will just end up proving yourself correct.

Just a friendly quote for you to remember: "If you think you can, or you think you cannot, you are absolutely correct."

- Henry Ford

Upholding positive thoughts that your presentation will succeed is a stepping stone towards it. Regardless of how stressful it might be, how high piling the expectations were, or how loaded the things needed are, you need to know how to effectively cope with these stressors.

Condition and talk to yourself. There is nothing bad with spending some introspective time with yourself. After all, who will be the first person you should trust? There's no other person in this world but you!

Tell this to yourself: "I can do this. I think I can, so I can absolutely can. I will deliver my talk successfully."

Words to Ponder

You need to believe in yourself. You need to believe in your strengths and capabilities that they will lead you towards better outcomes. Positive thoughts have a great benefit on your delivery. Thinking that this will be a noble and rare opportunity to share information, entertain people or become a change agent is a kind of mind-set that could make you an effective presenter.

But of course, mortals are not meant to be perfect. But what matters is that for you learn from such mistakes. An adequate formula of confidence for you to deliver well and enjoy what you are doing is already enough. There will be times when you will experience mistakes or shortcomings in life. Learn, move on, and improve! That's how it supposed to be.

Creating Effective Visual-Aids

Aside from a clean speech delivery, it is also important to prepare something for the eyes of your listeners. Studies showed that people tend to retain and understand the topic more through written words.

According to Edgar Dale's Cone of Experience Theory which provides percentages of the information retained on an individual's mind through various means, he claimed that people can retain 10% of the information when it is read, 20% when it is heard, 30% when it is seen, 50% when it is heard and seen, 70% when it is said, and 90% when it is said and done.

This implies how important it is to show something that will aid your audience to understand what you are pointing out. Doing all the talking without something to show will more likely decrease the chance of retaining what you have said and maintain their attention to you.

Therefore, it is very necessary to take note of the following reminders in creating your presentation:

1. For printed or hard copies of visual aids with numerous paragraphs, you can use serif fonts such as Times New Roman for readability. If you prefer to project your presentation, use sans serif fonts such as Arial especially if the font size is small.

2. In terms of your presentation design, some institution or organization requires a certain format or design to follow. Make sure to comply with it. Otherwise, if it is not compulsory, then you have the freedom to design it as creative, as appropriate, and as presentable as possible. But make sure not to overdo it because people's attention might get diverted to it and the message that you want to convey will be disregarded. Remember to choose an appropriate color scheme.

3. Do not use more than 2 different fonts and more than 2 text variants such as bold, underline, italic, on one text. It will look confusing and distracting.

4. Make sure that your texts are readable enough even up to the last row of your audience seated at the back. You can use 14-16 font sizes for your texts.

5. Do not overload your presentation with texts. You can just include there an outline of your important points or cues that you needed. Remember the 7-lines-per-slide rule.

6. Try to put some pictures, video clips or, sound clips that are relevant to your speech. Also, you can consider incorporating some inspiring or funny quotations to your introductions. It will help to make an impression that what you are going to say is important. You can use these techniques to catch the interest of your audience.

7. Use some presentation animations. Look how they will be amazed.

8. You can try to reproduce your presentation into a hard copy and disseminate it. This would be helpful to those people whose visions are not clear. However, the downside of this is, your audience might get distracted and not listens to you because anyway, they have on their hands what they need to hear.

Words to Ponder
Create your own cue cards and notes. Cue cards are especially useful for beginners who are new to presentation and public speaking. Ensure that they are simply written and are arranged accordingly to your purpose. It can aid you whenever you feel like you are forgetting something. Just do not always look at it during the entire presentation, else you might rely too much on it and lose your confidence in the presentation; same goes to the audience in you.

Chapter 8: Traits Of Good Public Speakers

Aside from casting out your fears and anxieties of public speaking, you must also know how to become a better speaker. To do that, you must learn about the traits that all great public speakers share. By reading this chapter, you should be inspired to learn more about public speaking and imbibe the traits that make the average public speaker a confident and effective communicator.

Now, as a public speaker, you must have been exposed to rules regarding your posture, eye contact, and gestures, as well as the tone and volume of your voice. You must have already heard how public speakers should always stand with their feet apart, their chests out, and their heads held high. While there is nothing wrong with these sorts of rules, they do not really tell you how to become a great public speaker. All they tell you is how you should look while speaking. Most of those rules are flexible anyway and so, you often end up wondering about what it really takes to move your audience and bring your message to the hearts of others without sounding too pretentious or well-rehearsed. Below is a list of traits that public speakers must have, for them to inspire their audience.

Good speakers are good listeners, too.

It's true. To be a good public speaker, you must be able to listen with sincerity and genuine concern for your audience. This means that you are fully aware of how the audience is taking your speech, and you know what to do to make them more comfortable or interested in what you are saying.

For example, the best speaker knows how to break the ice between himself and a foreign audience. That speaker may start with a joke, or may simply admit that he is nervous and hopes that his message strikes a chord in the audience though he may stammer or commit a few mistakes.

By listening to his audience's response, the speaker will know if his strategy was successful or not, and will be able to proceed to the next part of his speech, still adjusting it to the needs of his listeners.

Good speakers know their written speeches to the letter, but aren't afraid to adlib either. Sometimes, even the best constructed speech will not be enough to sway the crowd, or make them feel as enthusiastic as you are about your topic. Sometimes, the best way to beat public speaking anxieties, as well as bored listeners is to just go with the flow, and let your speech shape itself naturally. Knowing how to adlib if you forget your lines, or if you want to make a point, is a true advantage. This means you are more comfortable speaking to others and you are not completely dependent on your cue cards. This also means you have established a connection with the audience and you have become more than just an individual standing at the podium.

Good speakers are empathetic and sensitive to their audience.

The best speakers know which jokes are appropriate and which stories are fine to share. They know which anecdotes will help them with their message, and which ones they should avoid. As a good speaker, you should be empathetic to your audience. If you were in their place, would you like to hear what you are about to say? Would you be convinced of the stories, or laugh at the jokes you are about to share? How would you feel if you were in their shoes?

Know your audience and respect them—because without them, you and all the other public speakers will no longer be needed.

Good speakers do not like what they do—they love what they do!

Yes, for someone who has fears or anxieties related to public speaking, being passionate about convincing or inspiring a crowd can be hard to achieve, but it isn't impossible. With practice and determination, hard work and focus, there is no doubt that you will soon fall in love with the thrill and fulfillment that only public speaking can bring. Don't worry if you can't find the strength to love your craft just yet. But stay positive. Whenever your fears block you from becoming a better speaker, remember what you love about public speaking in the first place, remember your audience, your message, and your chance to move others. Keep all those things in mind, and pretty soon you'll find yourself in love with the art of public speaking.

Chapter 9: Confidence

No matter how interested and experienced we may be in public speaking, anxiety cannot be avoided. We experience it especially as the day of the speech gets closer. We start to ask questions that make our stomachs churn. For example: Will the audience like me? Will my mind go blank when I begin to speak? Have I prepared adequately?

If the thought of delivering a speech makes you nervous, you are not alone! According to a commonly quoted survey, more people are afraid of public speaking than they are of dying. People who experience a high level of apprehension while speaking are at a great disadvantage compared to more conversational, confident people.

Individuals who confidently express themselves are viewed as more competent. They also create a better impression during job interviews and are more likely to be promoted than apprehensive people.

Confidence develops a positive impression while anxiety creates a negative one. When we speak, we are communicating in three ways - verbally, visually, and vocally. Our verbal delivery may be clear and well organized; but when we are anxious, the audience will likely notice more our negative vocal and visual signs (for example, lack of eye contact, poor posture, hesitant delivery, and strained vocal quality). Yet, when we are confident and our verbal, visual, and vocal signals are in unity, we look more credible.

If we want people to believe us when we speak, if we want to improve the impressions we make, we need to boost our confidence. This chapter will give you some tips on how to manage speech anxiety to give more confident and professional deliveries.

Call it speech anxiety, stage fright, or communication apprehension; you have to understand it for numerous reasons. First, speech anxiety can incapacitate you. Second, misconceptions about it can strengthen your anxiety. Finally, knowing the strategies for managing speech anxiety can help lessen your apprehension.

Factors Contributing to Speech Anxiety

Speech anxiety is not new – it's been around for as long as people have been talking to one another. Most speakers who have experienced speech anxiety know the importance of being calm and confident when speaking.

Some feel nervous while others stay calm and relaxed when speaking. Factors in speech anxiety differ from person to person. But general factors apply to all of us.

Knowing the causes of speech anxiety is the first step in managing it effectively. Many anxiety-generating factors affect nearly all of us, including:

• Poor preparation
• Inappropriate self-expectations

- Fear of evaluation
- Excessive self-focusing
- Fear of the audience
- Not understanding our body's reactions

Misconceptions about Speech Anxiety

No one would agree that experiencing speech anxiety is enjoyable. However when we better recognize why our bodies respond as they do, we become more prepared to face our anxieties.

Let us examine some misconceptions and how to counter them.

Myth / Misconception   Reality

1. Everyone will know if a speaker has speech anxiety. Few, if any, will notice. So keep the secret to yourself and start acting confident.

2. Speech anxiety will intensify as the speech progresses. It's all up to you. Mostly, a well-prepared speaker will relax as the speech progresses.

3. Speech anxiety will ruin the effect of the speech. If you let it, it will. On the

contrary, speech anxiety may improve a speaker's effectiveness.

4. The audience is inherently hostile and will be overly critical of what we do. Most listeners are polite especially when the speaker is obviously trying to do well.

Strategies for Managing Speech Anxiety

Every speaker has to know the different strategies available for managing speech anxiety. As you give speeches, you learn strategies that work especially for you. Let's look at some strategies that have been very effective to many speakers.

1. Be Well-Prepared and Practice Your Speech.

Nothing can make you feel more anxious than knowing that you are not well prepared. After all, isn't your anxiety all about looking stupid in the eyes of your audience? Poor preparation will guarantee this.

To prepare adequately, first, try to know your listeners beforehand (if possible) and organize your speech and visual aids for this specific group.

Next, prepare easy-to-follow notes. Using these notes, practice your speech three or more times from start to end – speaking out louder each time. Mentally thinking through your speech is not the same thing as actually speaking in front of the audience. For instance, if you will be standing during your speech, stand while practicing. If you will be using visual aids, practice using them. As you practice, time yourself to check if you have to shorten or lengthen the speech.

Lastly, expect possible questions and prepare answers for them. Knowing that you are well prepared will help lessen much of your apprehension.

2. Warm Up First.

Speakers are no different from singers who warm up their voices, musicians who warm up their fingers, or athletes who warm up their muscles before a performance. Before giving a speech, you'll need to warm up your voice and loosen your muscles. Various techniques can help you do this. For instance, try singing up and down the scale, the way singers do before a concert. Read aloud a note or a page from a book, changing your volume, pitch, rate, and quality. Do some stretching exercises such as touching your toes and rolling your head from side to side. Practice different gestures such as pointing, pounding your fist, or shrugging your shoulders. Just like musicians and athletes, these warm-up exercises will help you relax and will make sure that you are prepared to present at your very best.

3. Use Deep Breathing.

One fast way to calm your anxiety is through deep breathing. This involves taking in deep breaths through your nose, holding it while you count to five, and then slowly exhaling through your mouth. As you exhale, think that the pressure and nervousness are slowly draining down your arms and out your fingertips, and down your body and legs and out your toes. Repeat the procedure a second or third time if necessary.

4. Prepare an Introduction That Will Relax You and Your Audience.

Most speakers find that once they get a favorable audience reaction, they will relax. This is why several speakers begin with humor – it relaxes them and their audience. If a humorous introduction is improper or you are uncomfortable with humor, sharing a personal experience is another alternative. Whatever you prefer, make your initial moves work so you can feel comfortable throughout your speech.

5. Focus on Meaning.

Rather than worrying about how you look or sound, or about whether you are impressing your listeners, focus your energy on getting your meaning across to your audience. In other words, be sure your listeners are following the order of your speech and understanding your ideas. Pay close attention to their nonverbal feedback. If they look confused, explain the concept again or add another example. A speaker who is focusing on the audience soon forgets about being anxious.

6. Use Visual Aids.

Visual aids (Chapter 10) make listening easier for your audience and increase your confidence as a speaker. They make it practically impossible for you to forget your main points. If you're unsure of the next point, just put up your next visual aid. Moreover, using visual aids such as posters, flipcharts, or actual objects not only can add eye-catching movements to your presentation, but can also keep you fully engaged in your presentation, so you'll be bothered less by your appearance.

7. Develop a Positive Mental Attitude.

With positive imagery, you develop a positive, vivid, and detailed mental image of yourself. When you visualize yourself speaking confidently, you become more confident. In your mind, you can simulate feelings (of pride, for instance) even when no real situation exists. Obviously, positive imagery alone will not give you the outcome you want unless you prepare and practice your speech.

Positive self-imagery can be used in many aspects in life. It can help us manage apprehension in job interviews, problem-solving discussions, testing situations, or any circumstances in which our confidence needs a boost.

To succeed in public speaking, you have to visualize yourself as a successful speaker. No amount of talk, encouragement, or practice will make you successful if you deem yourself an anxious or ineffective speaker.

Chapter 10: Your Image

There are several areas of your image that need to be discussed. Most of them have little to do with your appearance. All of them have to with your qualities. All of them will affect how receptive the audience is to your speech.

Dress to Impress

The first thing you want to do is to dress to impress your audience. However, this doesn't mean that you need to dress to the nines every time you come

out on stage. How you dress will be entirely dependant on the event and the audience that attends. You need to dress in such a way that your audience connects to you. This may very well mean that you need to wear a tuxedo

or formal clothing.

The most common mode of dress is in sharp business attire with every detail in place. However, sometimes you may need to be a little more casual, such as a speech for a university extension co-op that is held at a fairgrounds building.

Whatever style in which you dress, you must attend to some of the more common details every time, for every audience. Always be clean and smelling nice. Always have you hair freshly cut or styled. Always have your clothes pressed. Always keep your teeth impeccably clean. Always have breath fresheners handy (sprays or strips that melt right away; not gum, candy, or lozenges). Always have your hands and fingernails clean with the cuticles pushed back. Ladies, shape and polish your nails. If you're wearing
open-toed shoes, get a pedicure.

These might sound like something that anyone would take into consideration, but people can get in a hurry and forget. In fact a lot of people forget the small details that people take notice of and this has an impact on them. Make yourself a checklist of what you're going to wear and when you're going to shower, and go right on down the line of all the details you need to do before you leave.

Arrive Early

Show up at least 60 minutes prior to an engagement. An event planner will normally take care of any detail that needs to be in place ahead of time, like microphones. Nevertheless, sometimes that doesn't happen, and you need to make sure that you have the necessary equipment set-up and ready to go.

Along with the stage set-up, you need to be ready to talk with the people who have asked you to speak. They may have invited you to speak, but it's your job to make them feel comfortable and positive. You also want to get an idea of any other outcomes they want that they may have not stated. This doesn't always happen, but occasionally there may be concerns or agenda's that were not stated up front. You may need to make alterations in your speech
to accommodate them.

Prepare Mentally and Physically

You want to have time to prepare yourself mentally and physically to speak. This may take anywhere from a few seconds to a few minutes. The more

you speak, the more you'll know what you need to do for self-preparation.

Be sure to smile. At everyone. Smiling is one of the easiest ways to make connections with people. You want people to relate to you so that they will be more receptive to your message. Smiling will break down barriers and make you more approachable.

On Stage All the Time

You are on-stage all the time. Everyone you meet will judge you and your message by how you conduct yourself both on and off stage. I've seen speakers that were full of passion and aroused audiences' emotions to a fever pitch. However, when they were out-of-sight from the public, they were surly and difficult. This kind of behavior poisons your presentation and your reputation. Make no mistake; what the folks behind the scenes see and hear is just as important as the audiences' observations.

We talked about your body language in preparing to give your speech. The body language you portray both before and after the speech is just as important. Your body language will say a lot about your level of confidence and professionalism. The same rules apply: good posture, relaxed shoulders, good eye contact, smiling, hands to your sides.

Voice control is another detail of your image that you need to monitor. When rehearsing your speech, listen to your voice. Are you loud or soft-spoken;

do you speak in a monotone or have tonal inflections that convey your meaning? Before your speech, work with the person handling the soundboard. Check the sound levels, making sure that you speak like you would normally speak during a speech. Be emphatic and bring your voice

down; make sure the sound person hears how your voice modulates so they can adapt the sound to match your voice.
Modulating the volume of your voice from public speaking to speaking with
the public is also important. Have you ever heard someone who speaks over the rest of the crowd? They sound pretty awful, don't they? As a public speaker, your natural instinct will be to project your voice. When you're speaking one-on-one, make sure you keep your boom-box voice at bay.
The delivery of your speech is also an important part of your image. You'll want to speak your best no matter if the audience is a group of business people or an assembly hall of collegians. Answer the questions of why, what, how, and who. Know who your audience is, what they already know

and want to know, why they want to hear your input, and how you're going to present to them. Work through the logical sequence in your outline that you've customized for just this audience.

Your delivery should be dynamic and hypnotic. This type of delivery requires both study and practice. However, this work will pay off in the end. You'll lead them to your inescapable conclusion; and satisfy the needs of your clients as well. For you, that translates into more bookings, and more income.

One caveat: I recently read an article where Dr. Gary S. Goodman, President of www.customersatisfaction.com, spoke about a delivery style that completely goes against conventional wisdom.

Gary was in the Navy and was a part of a select few chosen to train senior Navy managers. Gary was already a professional speaker. However, an officer, who appeared to have little to no speaking skills, was his trainer.

His trainer did everything wrong, delivery-wise. From hemming and hawing, to talking in a monotone voice, he lacked any kind of dynamics. He used all kinds of colloquialisms that you wouldn't think would fly. He came across like a version of Tom Hanks and John Wayne mixed together.

The real kicker came when the evaluations came in - this guy consistently rated the highest of all the speakers within the group. Always.

After studying the evaluations and the training results that followed, Gary found the trainees loved the character this guy had adopted. The trainees enjoyed the persona that he used and the easy way he presented the material. In the end, even the most difficult and hardened of the Navy managers were successfully trained in the techniques that the Navy wanted them to learn.

Gary adopted this style of delivery. He states that he is able to make a seven-figure income from using this delivery style.

Find a Role Model

Finally, think about Importance of having a role model. "A role model? How does having a role model help me become a great speaker?"

Role models help us learn the things that we want to learn and become. A role model will inspire, teach, and show how to live a better life. They can teach us to save us time and money through listening to their wise words. They can help us find direction in life.

The top speakers on the market have role models they pattern themselves after. They will attest to how their role models helped them to be a success in life as well as a successful speaker.

If you want to be a great speaker, take the time to learn from other great speakers.

Abraham Lincoln, Theodore Roosevelt, Winston Churchill, Dr. Martin Luther King, Jr., John F. Kennedy. These men are noted in history for their character and how that character came out whenever they spoke. Their words still inspire and urge us to be better human beings that live with integrity.

A role model will help us to gain confidence in ourselves. When we pattern ourselves after a person that we admire, we hold a mirror up to our lives to watch for growth. When we see this growth occur, we become more confident in ourselves and shed another layer of fear.

Think about whom you consider a great person. What is it about their life that makes you have this opinion? Are they a person with great integrity? Are they the best in their field? Are they a great athlete? Are they the funniest person you've ever heard? Whoever this person is, start studying

their life. Look at their failures as well as their successes. Learn what things
will be valuable for you to adopt, and what things they do that you want to

avoid. Implement the good things and throw out the bad. You'll find that starting new endeavors, like public speaking, will be a little easier.

You've made a foundation to build upon, so accomplishing difficult things, like public speaking, becomes nothing more than an exercise in growth.

Chapter 11: How To Improve Your Public Speaking Skills

Hopefully, after a couple of weeks you may have conquered your fear of public speaking. From this point forward, all you have to do is to improve on your speech delivery so that slip-ups that lead to a relapse of your fears will not happen.

Here are some helpful tips that will take your oratorical skills to the next level:

Prepare your introduction

In most, if not all speaking events, an emcee will introduce you to the audience.

You should provide your own introduction, rather than letting him or her use a general one for ushering you onto the stage.

Write down a short, but detailed introduction about yourself; around 100 to 150 words should be more than enough. List your qualifications in bullet points, not in paragraph form so the emcee can have some leeway for ad-libbing. In the end, add "Please join me in welcoming [your name]," this will serve as a signal to the audience to applause your entrance. The praise will help boost your confidence and scare away most of your stage fright.

Know your audience

Unless you will be speaking in front of the shareholders of a company that is about to go bankrupt, and then you can safely assume that your audience will not be that hostile against you. However, just to be on the safe side, study your audience in advance so you will be able to adjust your speech according to what they want to hear.

For instance, if you will be addressing a room full of high school students, it will be in your best interest to keep the technical terminologies down to a minimum. Even if you are delivering your speech in an upbeat and light-hearted manner and your audience cannot understand one word that you say, they will get bored.

Look for an on stage persona and stick with it

If you take a look at some of the most famous public speakers, you will find that their personas when they are on the stage seems somewhat different than when they are speaking one-on-one. You need to find this slightly more extroverted part of yourself and use it whenever you need to address a crowd of people. Everybody has a talkative side; you just need to find and get in touch with yours.

It is not to say that you have to be someone you're not, you just need to be someone a bit better than you typically are. You do not have to undergo some drastic change like adopting a different manner of speaking or acting, just accentuate your positive characteristics and minimize your negatives.

Don't stay stationary

When you are delivering your speech, it is best if you were to walk around a bit on the stage instead of hiding behind the lectern. Use the space provided to you; walk towards the edge so that the people not seated in the center aisles will feel know that you are also talking to them.

Open your speech using a story

Before you get on with the meat and potatoes part of your speech, you need to get your audience warmed up using a touching story related to the subject of your speech. For instance, if you're speaking at a career convention, tell the story of how you stumbled upon the career you have right now. Your story does not have to be factual in order to be effective. You can tell a fictional story on how a family was able to survive a harsh winter with the help of a certain product; a product that is similar to the one you are offering.

Prepare your speech, but don't memorize it

Most people, when asked to deliver a speech, would write down their entire address on a piece of paper and remember it word-for-word. You should avoid doing this if you want to become an effective public speaker. Instead, divide your speech into several parts and explain the parts in the most natural manner you can.

When preparing your speech, you should write down the details using bulleted lists. Arrange the items on your list, so they make sense when you explain them one at a time. To make things easier for you to understand, imagine your entire speech as a house with multiple rooms, each room symbolizing the different parts of the topic you will be discussing, and take the audience on a guided tour of the house by ushering them into the different rooms.

Do a trial run of your speech if possible

Ask the organizers of the event if it is possible for you to inspect the venue and make sure that everything is perfect for your speech. Most of the time, the organizers will give you permission as long as you don't hinder their preparations.

If you will be presenting a couple of slides, make sure that the projector works perfectly. Also, make sure that the operator of the projector already has a copy of your presentation, and tell him or her to check if your file runs on the computer. Even if your presentation ran just fine on your computer at home, do not assume that it will also work with a computer at the venue.

Check if the lights would not blind you when you are on stage, and check if their microphones are in good working order. These kinds of preparations may seem too much for some people, but it is better to be safe than sorry, especially if you are risking making a fool of yourself in front of a crowd.

Engage your audience

One of the best ways to keep your audience's attention is to ask them for their opinions on the subject of your talk. They don't even need to provide you with an answer; you can just look at them and ask them a question.

What to do when you mess up

It does not matter how many times you have delivered speeches; you will mess up every now and then. In the beginning, you might have become paralyzed when you realize your mistake, but now you are more confident with your public speaking skills and able to rebound a lot quicker.

If and when you do screw up while delivering a speech, and you actually feel that most of the audience is not on your side, look for that one face in the crowd who seems to be enjoying your speech. It does not matter how much you screwed up your speech, there will at least be one person in the crowd who is on your side, find out where he or she is and look for any sign of support that will help you boost your confidence.

Bonus tip: always have a glass of water within reach when reciting a speech. You will be talking endlessly for ten minutes or more, so your throat will surely get dry. Take a sip of water now and then to prevent your voice from cracking and ruining the momentum you already have gone.

Follow these tips, so you can be sure that you will not relapse back to the days when you would shrink at the thought of speaking in front of other people. You can now say that you have gained control over your glossophobia and have become that which you have always wanted to be: a confident and strong-willed public speaker.

Chapter 13: Change Your Mindset About Public Speaking

In addition to pinpointing your fears and examining them, the other key to overcoming your fear of public speaking is changing your mindset from a negative to a positive one. Although this does take work, there are some exercises that can help you achieve this.

Practice

The best way to become a confident and skilled public speaker is to practice. This includes practicing before giving a speech so that you are prepared and also just doing more public speaking. The more you do, the more confident you will become. You may even get to the point where you welcome the opportunity to get up in front of a group of people to speak because you realize all of the benefits that go along with it.

Breathing Exercises

Another thing that you can do to really help calm yourself down and focus on the positive is to do deep breathing exercises. Of course you will want to do this right before your speech to help relax you, but you can also do deep breathing exercises on a regular basis as you are preparing your speech to help get you in a more positive frame of mind. When we are anxious, our breathing tends to be rapid and shallow. Learn how to practice deep and slow breathing to calm yourself down. This will help you feel more in control and help to relax you.

Visualization

Being able to visualize your success is also key to overcoming your anxiety about public speaking. Visualize yourself as a confident and engaging speaker. See your audience in your mind laughing at your jokes, nodding in approval and giving you a big round of applause at the end of your talk. Really think about what the consequences will be of giving a successful speech.

Visualization is key to overcoming your fears and negative attitudes and replacing these with positive thoughts. From the moment you know you are going to be giving a speech, start to practice visualization. Have a clearly defined goal for your speech and visualize the outcome that you desire. This will go a long way towards changing your attitude from being fearful and negative and thinking that the worst will happen, to one that is confident, relaxed, positive and looking forward to achieving your goals. This does take practice, but it is so well worth it to change your mindset. Use the tools of practice, breathing exercises, visualization and setting specific goals to turn your attitude and outlook around.

Chapter 14: The Close

Why we are going to the CLOSE now instead of the biggest and meatiest part of the three golden guidelines.

We have dealt with the OPEN. Hopefully you have followed the system and can now OPEN about anything!

Or maybe you are still wrestling with it - but you are on the way so keep practicing.

As stated at the end of the last chapter, the OPEN and CLOSE are really the easiest parts. If you get those bits down to a fine art you are TWO THIRDS of the way there! How cool is that?

You are just over 30 pages into this book and you are already into the 'second third' of the magic formula.

Here is the next part of the magic formula for putting together a speech.

THE CLOSE.

Just like the OPEN and the BODY (which we will deal with soon) the CLOSE is a specific skill.

Once learned, not only with it be with you forever, but you will always finish on a high, leaving your audiences wanting more.

What is the key point and therefore the power in the CLOSE?

Just as you only get to make ONE FIRST IMPRESSION, you also only get to make ONE LAST IMPRESSION.

It is why the CLOSE is so important.

Like anything in life, it's how we remember the last thing someone said to you that leaves you with a lasting impression. Here's a few golden tips that will help you become a great closer.

THE CLOSE needs to be clean and crisp.

THE CLOSE needs to leave no doubt you have finished.

Here are some examples of the way we CLOSE in general life.

In a telephone conversation, when you are winding up, you generally says something like ...

"Hey thanks for the call, gotta go - yeah, bye"

When you bump into a friend at the mall, stop for a chat and it's obviously time to go and (in your own way and own words - everyone is different) you say something like...

"Well better get going now, great to see you. Catch up another time, bye".

If you are one of those cool dudes, it might go something like...

"Later dude" followed by a man hug with lots of back slapping!

You probably have your own special ritual for saying goodbye.

This is the point where a lot of new speakers have trouble … they don't know how to end.

What do I say? "Thanks for listening" and just leave?

Well you could do that, but this type of ending leaves the whole thing a bit flat and unfinished. Also the audience is not really sure when to clap.

Big applause, fantastic ... you did so well ... great!

Solid applause, you did pretty well so be happy with that response.

Lame applause, Good going but let's see if we can do better next time!

When you hear the crickets at the end and the audience is silent with their arms folded across their chests, you know you still have a bit of work to do!

The CLOSE is quite easy when you know how to do it. Generally when I close a speech (a 'speak') it is always finished with ...

"Thank you for allowing me to speak today and may I leave you with this final thought"

(Which leaves no room for anything else in the audience's mind except this is the finish)

My final thought is nearly always centered on leaving a 'gift' of some kind. This one works almost without fail.

"THANK YOU ladies and gentlemen. Allow me to leave you with this final thought ... when you speak from the heart, there are no mistakes."

I really love that CLOSE.

I encourage to not only learn this line but use it freely as YOUR close if it will help you.

You could, if you wanted to beef it up a little to give it more impact by saying...

"Thank you ladies and gentlemen, you have been a great audience and I thank you for listening to me today and allowing me to share my story with you.

The final thing I would like to share with you is a golden secret I learned when I first started out speaking and has always given me courage...

(Then take a little pause to build anticipation)

...When you speak form the heart, there are NO mistakes. Thank you".

Then you wait for the applause!!!!!

This is a very strong finish and leaves a positive lasting impression on your audience.

Here's a few other examples of how you could CLOSE neatly and 'cleanly'.

"Well ladies and gentlemen, thanks so much for listening to my story - I hope you enjoyed it. I'll see you next time."

ANOTHER ... "That's about all I have to tell you about tonight, I hope you enjoyed hearing about my buddies who put their life on the line for me. Thanks very much!"

ANOTHER ... "Just before I go I would like to thank the committee for inviting me to speak about (whatever you spoke about) - I hope you enjoyed it. Thanks for having me."

ANOTHER ... "Ladies and gentlemen, it sure was a pleasure being able to speak with you tonight. I hope you enjoyed it, thanks a lot."

ANOTHER ... "Ladies and gentlemen, that's about all I have to share with you. I hope you are taking more home with you than what you came in with. It was a real pleasure to speak with you today. Thanks very much for having me!"

Think of the close as a wrap up in your own words. Very soon, you will come up with your own favorite close. As I said earlier, a helpful hint maybe to take clues from how you wrap up your own conversations in person or on the phone.

Whatever you come up with, just make sure your audience clearly understands that it is the CLOSE. You have finished with zero room for misunderstanding!

So the golden guidelines are hopefully now crystal clear.

The **CLOSE** is how you finish off cleanly.

The audience definitely knows you're done!

The **OPEN** is simply introducing yourself.

Sharing with your audience what you are going to be speaking about.

Well done. You are now officially two from two!

Now let's move on to the largest slice of the whole gig - THE BODY.

Chapter 15: The What

Where's the beef?

Some years ago--on second thought—**many,** there was a very popular commercial about a hamburger that looked great in the television advertisement but when the eager consumer--I believe it was a little old lady--received her purchase she opened the bun and cried in dismay, "Where's the beef?"

You don't want something similar happening with any speech you give, do you? This is where properly researching your topic comes into play so that your speech will have substance, and that it's not some skimpy hamburger patty that your audience can't sink their teeth into.

Okay, I know some speakers believe they can wing it, already having some knowledge of their topic, but they still need to organize their ideas, and not find themselves having to resort to padding and spouting irrelevant material.

Audiences recognize when speakers are trying **to get one over** them.

So in preparing your speech, let's assume you have finally decided to tackle the one on the game of cricket. First, you need to decide up front what angle to take. Are you going to talk about the history of the game or how to play the game, the rules of the game, great players of the game, or the time when the West Indies, in their glory days, dominated the game? While brainstorming, please be mindful of the amount of time you have been given for your speech and this will help determine your approach. You then decide what you want to put in or leave out depending on your knowledge of what the audience needs to know. You certainly don't want to add to your anxiety by not knowing what you are talking about. Know your material and help reduce those factors that can cause you to appear scattered and disorganized.

If your goal is to persuade the audience to change their attitude towards the game you need to ensure that the audience has enough information on your positives that make up your pro-stance. It would serve you well to include some opposing views to what you are proposing to show that you are aware of what people usually put forward as
 counterarguments and that you are on top of your game. For controversial issues, by including opposing views you are letting your audience know that you are not afraid of confronting known arguments from the other side, and your argument becomes even stronger when you have addressed these concerns yet show that your view comes out on top.

The language you use....

Knowing the type of audience you'll be talking to also plays an important role in deciding what language you use, how formal or how informal you can be. In a formal situation, undoubtedly, you have to remember the context and speak standard language which could be any language but let's restrict ourselves to English, here. You need to adhere to the rules of grammar. Sentence structure and subject-verb agreement are two critical problem areas for many.

Green verbs and ripe nouns....

That's a popular expression used in some countries to describe grammatical errors, namely, noun/subject and verb agreement. We might often use singular verbs for numbers, such as, "There's three reasons" and that can pass muster. But "people is" just doesn't cut it. Likewise, saying, "you was" or "they was," can cause you to lose credibility fast.

A common expression these days, "Me and my friends" or "Me and Jim" (Susie, Mike, etc.), seems to have slipped into the realm of acceptable grammar. But beware! It's grammatically incorrect. "Me" is the subject before the verb so it should be "I." The correct way should be "My friends and I...." "Jim and I...," etc. This error can suddenly show up in a speech as, "Me and my colleagues are...." instead of, "My colleagues and I...." Similar errors are, "I had went..." instead of, "I had gone...." "They had came..." instead of, "They had come...." "Her and Eric..." instead of, "She and Eric...."

Slippery Language

Some speakers come to the podium and you get the impression that they are running a race. We have already acknowledged that public speaking is very stressful. As a result, far too many speakers race through their speech with one goal in mind--to finish as soon as possible. In the process they don't spend enough time articulating or pronouncing their words properly.

What you are doing is slipping and sliding through your words rather than taking the time to say them. Pay attention to your ending consonants in words, such as those ending in **g** or **d** or beginning with **th,** and so on. So take time to pause. Otherwise, it's as if you are sliding down a hill—a slippery slope. And you know how that ends--yes, in disaster.

Now to another analogy: When rushing through your speech you often find yourself, in your hurry to leave the podium, omitting key definitions and explanations of some of the terms and expressions you have used in your speech. You are as slippery as the figure skater who wants to get off the ice and so rushes through her program, failing to complete some of her jumps because of not enough preparation going into them--and falling down. The consequences of her actions? She receives a poor score, and the audience is cheated from really getting into her program. Give your audience time to "get into" your speech. And don't expect any high scores for your slippery language. It is affecting the clarity of your words and as a result your audience members miss a lot of what you are saying and can't really "get into" your speech.

Another look at "ers" and "ums" and "uhs"....

I believe that I can safely assume that many of you have heard of fillers such as "er" and "um" and "uh" and how to avoid them. Maybe addressing their overuse was one of the first criticisms directed at you while giving a speech.

Fillers are often due to nervousness and anxiety from speaking in front of an audience. They can be due as well to poor speech preparation or being very careful or extra cautious about what you want to say. Whatever the reason, your "ers" and "ums" and "uhs" might be habits of a lifetime and hard to break, so you need to pay attention and try to reduce, if not completely eliminate them.

Other fillers like, "y'know" "like" "kinda like" "sorta" and the overuse of "so" "so on and so forth" "basically" "pretty much" can be also a result of nervousness. For some speakers, however, it's a way of keeping the rhythm or cadence they are using in their speech so a word or phrase serves to fill the musical space to keep the rhythm going.

I'm a music lover, but not in this case. Stop the music, pause and listen to yourself. In rehearsing your speech, if you find yourself filling empty spaces with "er" and "um" and "uh" try beginning these vocalized pauses with a hard consonant such as **t** as in "ter" and "tum" and "tuh."

Vowel sounds like "um" and "er" and "uh," are much easier to slide into one of your pauses than those beginning with consonants, because of their degree of difficulty. Accordingly, you'll find that it's harder to slot in a "ter" or a "tum" in your empty space or pause, and the struggle to do so gives you some time to become aware that you are falling into the habit you are trying so hard to break.

Give this **uh** exercise a try.

Give this **tuh** exercise a try.

Notice the difference? Good. You're on your way.

Sloppy Language

What's sloppy language? It's my term for careless, indifferent-sounding language. Many speakers are unaware of this fault and unless someone points it out to them they will remain clueless.

"Stuff like that" "stuff" "and stuff" "whatever" "whatnot" "thing", "and everything" are some examples. "Y'know what I'm sayin" is another popular expression. The audience doesn't know what you are saying unless you say what you mean, and after a few of those "y'know what I'm sayin" (or "you know what I mean"), they just might not care to know. To me, it's a form of disrespecting your audience when you don't take the time to find the right word or phrase to express exactly what you want to say. Very unprofessional, I would say.

Cliches, slangs, and swearing can convey the same sense of unprofessionalism. You don't want your audience to think you don't have an original thought in your head, so avoid clichés or slangs. Slangs can be strategically used to engage a particular audience, especially a young audience, to let listeners know you're up with the latest and you understand **where they are coming from.** You have to be careful though, that you are up to date otherwise you might just become the butt of humor—unless you manage to work it into an icebreaking opportunity.

I'm also beginning to realize that many young people believe that "cool" is part of the standard vocabulary and not a slang. Well, it is. And I have news for you. Just because ""freakin" and "friggin" are not bona fide swear words, it doesn't mean that using them is acceptable in a formal context.

Never assume that the audience knows what you consider basic information even if some or many listeners might know. I remember once a speaker used the term "recidivism" in her speech and a member of the audience was overheard asking another, "What's that?" Feedback of this kind can be disconcerting and might throw you off your stride. So don't forget to define and explain your terms.

Use simple language to be clearly understood and stay away from **Mrs. Malaprop** and her blundering ways (There's even an **ism** named after her. Check it out). Simple language doesn't exclude similes and metaphors, analogies and other figurative language. Integrating language of this sort into your speech adds some color and imagination that can stir up your audience. Think of those great speeches, such as **I Have a Dream**, that have a special place in history. These speeches are known for their well-crafted language using some of the techniques found in a rich oratorical heritage that it would serve you well to learn more about.

Who knows? Maybe you have a speech inside of you waiting to be delivered then forever remembered.

Here are some more language types that I have created based on what I have heard in a variety of public speaking situations.

Sleepy Language

Are you familiar with the expression "sucking the oxygen from the room?" You don't want to be the one responsible for sending your audience to sleep, so you have to be alert to situations where audience members appear bored, yawn, nap, throw frequent glances at the clock in the room or at their watches, or leave furtively through side doors. Now there might be a myriad of reasons for what their body language and actions seem to be telling you, so not taking any of this personally is always an option that allows you to remain unfazed and focused. However, in becoming an effective public speaker, self evaluation is an ongoing process. So think of some questions you might want to ask yourself such as: What are my sentences like? Are they too long? Am I using enough short sentences? Sentences that are too long can lead to confusion and disinterest, easily derailing your message. Short sentences add energy but you have to be careful about overusing them and coming across as too simplistic. Practice varying the length of your sentences.

Listen to yourself to see if you are speaking in a monotone—that is, with no variety in your tone, or pitch. Vary your tone and aim for a lively expression on your face to show that you are really "into it" otherwise your audience might think you are sleeptalking.

Slimy Language

Many books on public speaking suggest using wit and humor to grab and maintain your audience's attention. That's all well and good, but like everything else in life you have to know where to draw the line. Pay attention to boundaries. A speech is not an opportunity to bat eyes at your audience, fiddle with your hair and flirt with members of the audience. It is not the occasion to test your skills as a stand-up comedian (unless it's that kind of speech) or sprinkle your speech with sexual innuendoes.

Sometimes flubs seem to come from nowhere. But they can be related to going **off message**, i.e., going off your script which can be coming from nervousness and anxiety or, ironically, from feeling too comfortable with your audience. Of course, it's unrealistic to expect to go through life without offending **somebody.** But being aware of what terms are offensive to groups, cultures, etc., is a big plus. Check your speech for cringe-inducing elements. And stay on message.

Chapter 16: Practical Steps To Manage Public Speaking Fear

It's not difficult to overcome the fear of speaking in public. There are many practical steps that one can be take to help to overcome it. The first step is to try and accept the fear so that you can understand its nature and know how it works. Do not fight the feeling. Instead, gain an understanding of how your fear affects your mood and disposition and find ways to conquer it. Your fear is likely to pass more easily if you come to terms with it and know how to deal with it. If your goal is to become an effective public speaker then it is important to overcome your fear. The advice that follows can help you to turn the situation around and overcome your fear of speaking in public.

Be Prepared And Ready

Preparation is the key to a successful speech. So, always prepare well and ahead of time, giving yourself some time to rehearse your speech.

Prepare well and ahead of time

Being prepared doesn't mean you have to be perfect. What is important is that you have prepared well and are ready, as this will make you less fearful of making a mistake. Preparation helps to focus your mind, so that you can concentrate on the points or ideas you want to convey, or share with your audience. However, you would be surprised at how many people overlook this important step.

In preparing, find out what is expected of you, so that you can plan an approach. Giving considering to factors such as the demography and cultural differences will help to determine the approach you take. Of course, your approach will also depend on whether your speech is to be a formal or informal one. Next, decide on the topic or points you wish to convey to your audience. Then do some reading and, if necessary, also do some research. This will equip you with valuable information with which to prepare your speech. However, do not over-prepare for your speech. Pace your preparation: don't try to take in too much information all at once. Limit the points or ideas you wish to use to that which you can comfortably handle. Trying to memorise and use a lot of facts and figures in a speech can sometimes cause confusion. This can produce added pressure, making one feel more fearful. Also avoid memorising your speech word for word. Instead, write down the points you wish to cover and base your reading around those points. Of course, you can make a list of the points you wish to raise and refer to those during your speech. You may also find it useful to prepare a mental outline of the things you want to say, so that you have a clear picture of the points you wish to focus on.

Being prepared will help you to get your message across in the most concise and comprehensible manner possible. You are also less likely to be distracted by the fear of making a mistake.

Practice Makes Perfect

Practising your speech is a very beneficial exercise. Practice and you will learn to master the art of public speaking. Practice until you feel you are ready to deliver your speech. You will be able to iron out any flaws in your speech and make any additions or amendments. But the more you practice, the more confident you will feel about delivering your speech, and it will help you to gain mastery of your topic. So, practice sufficiently, until you feel comfortable about standing in front of your audience and delivering your speech. Even when you are not about to speak in public, try to practice occasionally, to help retain and improve upon your public speaking skills. In addition, enlist the help of those around you. Rehearse your speech in front of family members, friends or colleagues and ask for feedback. You can use any constructive criticisms from those you know are trying to help you, to improve your speech. If you wish, you could also practice your speech in front of a mirror.

Exercises To Regain Composure

Before you walk on stage or stand up to deliver your speech, enter a room to facilitate a meeting or simply speaking at social gatherings or events, the first thing to do is to relax and free your mind of thoughts that are the cause of your fears. To control feelings of anxiety or nervousness, calm yourself by using deep and gentle breathing exercises, to help you gain composure. Taking deep, slow, gentle breaths helps to relax the mind and body and reduces the rate of heartbeat.

This also improves blood circulation to the brain and relaxes the nerves. Support your breathing by thinking of positive thoughts and images: this will also help you to relax and clear your mind so that you can focus on delivering your speech.

Grab Every Opportunity To Speak In Public
Exploit every opportunity to practice and help overcome your fear of speaking in public. You can condition yourself to speak in public by practising in front of friends or colleagues. There are usually opportunities at social gatherings and events. At work, volunteer to present a gift or say something complimentary about a departing friend or a colleague. At social events, make a point of standing up and saying something complimentary about the event. You could say a few complimentary words, giving credit to the host or organisers of the event, thanking them for their dedication and the hard work that has made the event enjoyable and a success.

Lead The Toast

Why not take the opportunity to lead the toast at social gatherings and events? If someone has already taken the initiative in leading the toast, then you could take the opportunity to reply to the toast. But base your comment on something not covered by the first speaker, which fits the occasion.

Chapter 17: Public Speaking Is Easy... It's All In Your Mind!

How should we define public speaking in our minds? Public speaking really is any speech performed in the open and not private – usually to an audience of one or more. Would you define a job interview as public speaking? Yes it is.

One of my students shared that because she did the public speaking course she was able to represent herself with ease and confidence at an interview that won her the job! Yes a job interview is a public speaking event.

Get the truth about public speaking straight in your minds:

Public Speaking is a mental process

Public Speaking is a practice

Public Speaking is a habit

Public Speaking is a performance

Once you understand the above statements of truth about public speaking you can now begin to address your fears and your concerns on such an activity.

The mind is the house of all fears, faith, and confidence. If you train your mind to become an effective speaker, you would have overcome your fears and stumbling blocks.

Public Speaking is a mental process

What are some of the things going through your mind as you get up to do a speech?

Are you wondering if you are prepared enough? Are you wondering if you are qualified enough to speak? Are you thinking about the mistakes you might make? Are you thinking about who is in the audience? Are you worried that you will be boring? Are you worried about how you look?

If these are some of the worries plaguing you as you attempt to do your speech, your body will register these worries and fears in nervousness, butterflies in the stomach and a dry mouth. If however you have been doing the exercises I spoke about in the earlier chapters, half if not all of your worries and fears will dissipate.

If you have been improving your vocabulary through reading widely and word collection, if you have been doing your breathing exercises, if you have been treating your body right with healthy eating and exercising you are prepared for the next level of tackling the tricks your mind plays on you.

If you understand your fears and realize that there are ways to overcome them by becoming conscious and training yourself to be prepared you will not experience a high degree of fear. What you will experience is anticipation, excitement and exhilaration. But you must do the work.

Forget about what happened to you when you were 10 years old or that which happened 10 years ago; forget about what happened when someone told you that you couldn't make it; forget about your past and whatever might be holding you back from shining. Create a positive mental attitude about how you want to be as a public speaker.

Visualize, and imagine yourself as a successful speaker, especially because you have done all the work necessary. I have not yet spoken about how to

go about writing your speech, but that will come later on; first you must get the right mental attitude.

You already know many things about many things – you just think you don't because you have not been asked to speak up. You can test what you know about 'cheese'. In your notebook; why not write a 100-word speech, without any research, just based on your knowledge alone? Do it in 5 – 10 minutes, see what you come up with. When you look you see that your mind is prepared to take on any subject, you just were not conscious of it.

Public Speaking is a practice

Never pass up an opportunity to speak up in public!

It might be at a meeting and the time has come for the question and answer period. Get up to the microphone and ask a question. At home in private, read aloud so that you get accustomed to hearing the sound of your own voice. You may be at a social event, start a conversation about something interesting with someone. Volunteer to read for children at a home, or a school or at the library – children are not harsh critics!

It would be hard to wait until you are called upon at the last moment to give a speech, if you have not been engaging in the practice of speaking in public on any topic.

As you begin to take more interest in reading widely, new ideas and opinions will occur to you to give you a basis for what you would speak on.

If you were to be interviewed by the media, how prepared would you be? Record yourself when you are doing your practice; it can be a video recording or an audio recording. That way you get used to what you sound like to others, and you are able to adjust the tone of your voice to suit your presentation.

Public Speaking is a habit

As public speaking is a practice, make it a habit. Be in the habit of doing all the things you know will help you in the process of becoming a good speaker.

Do not let it slide for just one day. If you were learning to play the guitar, violin or the piano you would have to develop the habit of practicing every day.

Set some goals for developing your public speaking habit; write them down in your notebook and follow them. The tips have been given to you in each chapter so far. Just do it!

Public Speaking is a performance

Understand in your mind that public speaking is a performance!

You are always performing as a public speaker. This means you must be at the very best when you perform. To ensure that you perform at your best it is important that you engage in the mental process, make it a practice and develop the habits that will support you in this process. It will not happen overnight but it can happen in as little as two weeks! Over time you will improve dramatically as you continue your practice and your habits!

Chapter 18: Writing A Memorable Speech

Have you ever had a conversation with someone and for some reason you were so wrapped up in it? And in the course of that conversation, you felt this fire in your soul? That is what happens when you have memorable conversations; little sparks are ignited in your heart and you feel motivated, revived and even empowered. Now, the speech you give regardless of the setting, should be able to have the same impact on your audience. It is because of this need that a lot of people are scared to speak publicly, but you shouldn't have to share the same fate. With these tips you can write and deliver a speech that people will not forget in a hurry.

1. Be Yourself

Throughout this book, you would find that this phrase is consistent; be yourself. When you are talking to a large crowd, it is easy to give in to the temptation to become hypothetical. You would find yourself using phrases that are foreign to you and re-echoing quotes that make you sound more intelligent, more wise, more worldly... basically you want to be more. there's nothing wrong in using quotes every now and then. I mean I use quotes in this book, but when drafting your speech, it is a time for you to be vulnerable. Your speech has to capture your essence. Remember this is about sharing your perspective. Strive to remain authentic.

2. Know Your Message

Essentially this is for you to understand the core of your message. In an earlier chapter, I remember including a quote that says, 'if you cannot write your message in a minute, you can't say it in an hour'. If you don't know what your core message is, you would find yourself dancing around the bush when you are called to speak or even when you are in the process of writing it. Know the exact message you want to pass across and then build the content of your speech around this. The 'knowing' I am talking about goes beyond knowing the topic. It is you having a critical understanding of what you want to share.

3. Tell a Story

One of my favorite childhood memories is sitting by the fire during the cold winter months leading up to the holidays and sharing stories back and forth about our family and our history. I was able to understand more about our roots from the stories that we shared by the fire. These stories brought the characters and personalities from our past to life in the way that was so vivid and relatable. And this is what made those stories memorable. People are able to understand you better when you use stories to illustrate your point just as I did here right now. With stories, things move from a realm of theories to a realm of possibilities. And when things enter this realm, they become unforgettable.

All the tricks the people use involve including anecdotes that are funny. Humor has a way of penetrating the mind and getting your message across. But all in all, one important thing you cannot ignore is research. No matter how well informed you are on a particular subject, you must acknowledge that the world we are in evolves at the speed of light. So, you need to ensure that you are updated. Especially if you are going to be talking about technical issues. Be updated on the subject and questions, be updated on people's perceptions of the subject and most importantly be updated on the problems surrounding the issues as well as the solutions to them.

Task:

Do a research on data related to the topic that you are speaking on. Get facts and figures on how it will affect the people you would be talking to. When you have this data, try and translate it into relatable terms. Then figure out how to include it in your speech. This would make the content of your speech real to whoever is listening.

Chapter 19: Organizing Your Speech

A good speech doesn't just 'happen'. Even stand up comedians, who seem so naturally funny put a lot of time and effort into their performances. Like public speakers, their carefully crafted presentations are the combination of:

Good Ideas

Known Facts

Research

Note Preparation

Practice

You already know how to begin assessing your audience by focusing on the general idea (purpose of your speech) and the specific idea and the central idea or thesis statement. Now it is time to consider the structure of your speech.

Speeches have three distinct parts:

Introduction

Body
Conclusion
Outlining
Organizing the Speaking Outline
Startle the Audience
Reveal The Topic
Establish Credibility
Preview the Body of the Speech

A. Look at the research and try to find a way to organize your main points (chronological, spatial, topical, problem-solution, cause-effect).

B. You should have at least two and no more than four main points.

C. Try to keep the wording as similar as possible in all the main points, and state them in full sentences (not in fragments). Also, devote an appropriate amount of time to each one.

II. Next, Make Components of the Main Points with Sub-points

Look at the research that fits under each main point and come up with key ideas that belong to these main points. These will be your sub points. You need at least two sub points for each main point.

B. Sub-points can be in complete sentences or fragments.

III. Support Your Sub-points with Sub-Sub-points (your facts and examples)

A. You must have at least four sources, that will be cited on your Reference section at the end of your outline. These sources will help provide you with your sub-subpoints.

B. Make sure in the body of your speech you tell us where your information came from,and/or who said it, in other words, CITE YOUR SOURCES IN YOUR SPEECH.

C. Sources could be books, book chapters, magazine/newspaper articles, interviews with expert or knowledgeable individuals, www sites, or any other viable Internet sources or electronic media.

D. Examples you use for supporting your main points--can be personal experiences.

IV. Use Connectives Throughout Your Speech (refer to the connectives handout)

A. Know what transitions, internal previews, internal summaries, and signposts are, and
when to use them (see your Connectives Handout on the reverse side)!

B. Label and include all connectives in your preparation outline.

SPECIFIC GUIDELINES FOR AN INFORMATIVE SPEECH PREPARATION OUTLINE:

MAKE CERTAIN THAT YOU LABEL EVERYTHING! (All labels are in parentheses--include all labels)

Title/Topic

Specific Purpose: This is what your main points must support or prove. Tell me in one
sentence what the purpose of your speech is.

Central Idea/Thesis Statement: Summarize your speech/outline in one sentence. Should
clearly sum up all of your main points.

INTRODUCTION

I. (Attention Getter) This could be a story or anything you know will GRAB your audience's attention.

II. (Credibility Statement) Answer the question "Why should we listen to YOU?" Give some type of factual information or some reference that will show that you know what you are talking about. This could be the fact that you had a class on the topic, or that you have done a lot of research, or that you have first hand experience with your topic, or you are an expert, etc.

III. (Relevancy Statement) Tell your audience how your topic is relevant to them.

IV. (Preview) Briefly reveal your topic and state what your main points will be.

Be sure to use connectives (see your Connectives Handout)!!

TRANSITION: Transitions are used to go smoothly from one part/point of the speech to another.

(Include in your transitional statement the exact wording you will use in your speech)

BODY

I. (MAIN POINT 1) Your first main point goes here-it MUST be one complete sentence.

INTERNAL PREVIEW: of Subpoints (A, B, AND C) Go HERE (Include the exact wording of your
internal preview)

A. (SUBPOINT) You should have at least two subpoints under each
main point. This could be one complete sentence. You cannot
have an A without a B.

1. (SUB-SUBPOINT) This is where the specific examples
from your research are included to support your main
points. You can use quotes, examples, stories. Be sure
to cite all sources. If you have a '1.' you must have a '2..'

a. (Sub-sub-subpoint) Further examples and
information to support your subpoint.
b. If you have an 'a.' you need a 'b.'
2. SUB-SUBPOINT More of the above.
B. SUBPOINT
1. SUB-SUBPOINT
2. SUB-SUBPOINT
C. SUBPOINT (optional)
1. SUB-SUBPOINT
2. SUB-SUBPOINT
INTERNAL SUMMARY OF SUBPOINTS A, B, AND C GOES HERE (Include the exact wording of
your internal summary)
TRANSITION: A transition is used to go smoothly from the 1st Main Point to the 2nd Main Point.
(Include the exact wording of your transition)
II. Your second MAIN POINT goes here. Follow the same format that you used for the
first main point.

III. Your third MAIN POINT goes here. (The total number of main points is optional, however, three main points seems to be the number easiest to manage as a speaker, and the easiest to remember for your audience.)

TRANSITION: A Transition is used to transition smoothly from the body of your speech into the conclusion. (Include in your transitional statement your exact wording)

Chapter 20: Get Some Routine And Banish The Butterflies

You have planned for success, got through any perfection-related roadblocks and arrived at the venue fully prepared and ready for your presentation. Your pre-speech or presentation nerves may well be at their highest pitch right about now so let us look at developing a pre-speaking routine. I get nervous right before any event. Most speakers do. I find such a routine to be a reassuring, predictable and beneficial nerve-calming activity and I would recommend all speakers adopt them to reduce their nerves.

There is no right or wrong way to design such a routine. It could be one thing which does the trick for you or it could take a combination of activities. There is only one sure way to find out what works for you so get out there and just do it; try many different things and see what works for you. Never give up. Keep trying new things until something does work.

Because everyone is so different, there is little point my offering pre-speaking routines in the hope one of them suits you. What I will do is outline my personal pre-speech routine with the aim of giving you some ideas as to structure and content. This should help to get you off to a good start when designing your own. I will also mention some techniques which other professionals I know use prior to speaking.

I always try to get to a gig at least one hour before my bit starts. If it is a conference and I have the time I try to get there early enough to talk to, watch and hear the other speakers. This gives me a chance to tweak my material in case of any overlap. There's nothing worse than getting to a gig to find most of your material has been covered by someone else already. A well-organised event should prevent this but hey, stuff happens right. I hate being late for anything so arriving early always reduces my overall nerves level significantly. No one needs any extra nerves, do they? After introducing myself to any organisers present, the first thing I do when I get to any event, is get any equipment I have brought set up correctly.

If AV equipment other than your own is going to be in use, for example an amplification rig, projector and/or microphone(s), I will first make friends with the AV operator. This person can make or break you so get them on side and keep them there. Ask them what you can do to make their day easier and do not ever be a prima donna; trust me on this, you need them far more than they need you.

I always record my presentations using a digital recorder and a lapel microphone so setting this up will also be in my routine. This is a bit technical but if there is a proper mixing desk in use, and to simplify my setup, I can often connect my digital recorder to one of the desk auxiliary outputs and therefore just have one microphone in use; yet another reason to make friends with the AV specialist as they can advise on how best to do this. I also put up any material sales display banners and generally tour the stage if the option is available to me.

The reason I do the stage tour is to get a good feel for what is to come. I visualise my audience hanging on my every word as I deliver another excellent and well-received presentation. Once I have finished visualising my extended standing ovation (it is my book you know so cut me some slack here) I will also look for any lighting issues, creaking floor boards, electronic feedback zones, audience blind spots or any other speaker unfriendly scenarios I can identify. I cannot always fix them but if I know they are there I can often work around them.

As an example of what can sometimes go wrong, I recently spoke at an event with an audience of a little over one hundred people. It was a spacious room and a sound system was supposed to be in use. During set-up the pre-amplifier blew and with no spares that was it. The AV guy packed up and went home. It was to be just my voice or nothing. I am blessed with a strong voice, so we simply had the audience move their tables as close together as reasonably possible and I got on with the show. Onward and upward. Never give up and never surrender.

If I am using my own laptop, I will now set up my presentation software and ensure the overhead projector and sound system is working in sync with my equipment. If there is an AV operator present, they will often help with this task.

Equipment checks now completed, I will get a tea or coffee and quickly run through my cue cards, if I am using them, one last time. Then I will find somewhere quiet and simply chill out for five or ten minutes. I centre myself with some meditation techniques, do some breathing exercises to relax further myself then run through my personal state-management techniques.

I have now got my speaker head on.

As the audience begins to arrive, I will always try to meet with as many of them as possible to create some pre-speech engagement. They generally enjoy it and I get to see at least a few friendly faces in the crowd when I am starting to speak. I always take a last-minute visit to the toilet for obvious reasons then have a final discussion with my introducer to check they have my introduction notes and are happy with them. It is now simply a case of waiting to go on. When I am introduced I trigger my pre-loaded state-management anchor and I am in the spotlight once again doing my thing as only I can.

Other speakers I know take one or two different approaches.

Some listen to their favourite music to get themselves in the mood. Some repeat their favourite positive thinking mantra to themselves or they meditate. Some insist on taking a specific flavour of herbal teabag to make their on-stage drink with. I know one speaker who has their spouse ring them up just before they go on stage and tell them how brilliant they are. Seriously, but hey if this works for them so who am I to criticise.

I do not recommend this last one personally, but some people like to arrive at the last possible minute and go straight onstage. This approach can and does get the organisers stress levels rising towards the stratosphere but again, whatever works for them is the order of the day.

See what works for you and begin to build yourself a repeatable pre-speaking routine. I predict you will be pleasantly surprised when your stomach-churning nerves turn into simple anticipatory excitement and you go on with a smile to deliver a winning presentation.

Chapter action points

Design a pre-speech routine for yourself and try it out when you next speak or present in public.

What is that? No speeches planned? Why not? If you want to grow as a speaker and presenter, then you need to speak and present.

Try your local service clubs, try the local business and networking groups as they often want speakers. Why not run a free seminar for your clients to educate them on industry changes? They may even bring some guests who will turn into new clients. Try out your local Toastmasters International Club. Whatever you do you must get that platform time to grow better as a speaker and presenter.

What about standing up at your next department meeting and presenting your report from the front of the room. It will be scary, but you will get some great practice, some feedback and a lot of respect.

After you have tried your new pre-speech routine, what could you remove, improve or add to make it better?

What do other speakers you know do for their pre-speech routines? If you do not know then ask them.

Adjust as required and adapt it as you move forward.

Chapter 21: List Of Topics

Ideally, start with the things which are closer to them, which they would not find difficult to speak on.

For the beginners, the possible topics could be:

☐ **Describe their school**- What is good about the school? What can be worked on? How are the studies? The school policies? Any other School which they like and why?

☐ Ask them about their favourite teacher **and not-so favourite teacher**

☐ **Ask them how their friends are doing?** What is that quality of their friend which they admire the most in them? Which is the quality they dislike in them? Have they spoken to their friends about this? Would they like to talk to him/her about it? Why and Why not?

☐ **Talk to them** about their hobbies, their favourite ice-creams

☐ **Is your child studious?** Talk to them about their favourite Subject or chapter

☐ **Is your child a cartoon lover?** Don't stop the child from watching cartoons. Use it as an opportunity to make them speak about their favourite character, what did they learn and how will they implement in their life. Talk to them about a not-so favourite character of theirs too.

☐ **Is your child a technical genius**? Ask your child to help everyone learn new technical stuff. Our elders usually have a challenge with technical stuff. So, if they speak about the same in RWA/ Society meeting, their speech will not only help the family members but also others around. This will in turn help them to express themselves but also understand how to manage expectations and handle an audience.

☐ **Is your child good at describing pictures?** Work with them. Ask them to describe a picture, drawn either by them or by someone else. So many get shared these days on social networking sites. They can even write or narrate stories around these pictures. Encourage their creative genius. **CREATIVITY IS AN ART WHICH CAN BE LEARNED WITH PRACTICE**.

◻ If they fumble, don't intervene. Allow them think on their own. When time to share your feedback then help them with words to fill the gap.**BE THEIR COACH.**

◻ **Does your child love to write poems, stories, or articles?** Many good speakers use poetry and quotes to their advantage while speaking. The poems, articles and stories help anyone to express their emotions and aesthetics as to what is good about the world. Writers and poets have a different eye. They notice what no one else notices.

◻ What if your child loves to write comic stuff?

Encourage them not only to recite their poetry, narrate their stories and express their viewpoint in front of everyone. See, if you can get them published in a local magazine, newspaper, school magazine. Once published, they can start earning a small amount of money as well. This will encourage them further to work on their skills. You never know, when your child gets noticed and might be called to speak on a bigger platform one day.

☐ Ask them to describe a party they had been to. What did they observe and if they made any new friends at the party?

They can describe any of their uncles and aunts. Be open to listen to what they have to say. Sometimes, they will come up with such wonderful insights about the adult behaviour and the people around that we had not even thought of till now.

Encourage them to open and make new friends. This will help them to be able to talk to people openly.

☐ **Events in the family or at a friend's place?** Have a special section for kids and teens on stage. Ask your friends and relatives to arrange for the same as and when they have an event. This would encourage other kids in the circle too. Once you volunteer to support them with this initiative, they would willingly accept your proposal.

HELP OTHER CHILDREN TO GROW AS WELL TO HELP YOUR CHILDREN GROW. ENCOURAGE HEALTHY COMPETITION AND YOU WILL SEE THEM CURIOUS TO WIN THE WAR OF WORDS.

☐ **Do you want your kids to be the talk of the town? Use Anniversary or Birthday Party to** encourage your children to extend special wishes to their host/birthday girl/birthday boy on stage, help them write a script in their own words. They might even like to render a poem or song to wish them. Not to forget a small skit, dance or a role play in front of everyone. Not only would your host love the special effort of your kids, but others around would appreciate and speak highly of them as well. Other kids in the party would get encouraged too.

☐ **Theme Party?** You might like to give a topic to all the children in advance in the party, while extending the invitation so that the kids come well prepared. Preparation in advance will make them quite comfortable in front of their audience.

☐ Picnic, Get -togethers, Social Gatherings? **Special Section for CHILDREN is a MUST.**

When going for any picnic or any other similar occasion, ask all the kids to volunteer to participate. They can identify a leader amongst them who can then, coordinate and lead the entire Public Speaking section for all. So, give every child a chance to become a leader. This will help them to open with everyone and make friends easily, especially if the child is of shy nature and does not mingle with everyone. Later, these skills will come handy to them at the time when they appear for **GROUP DISCUSSION** and **MEETINGS** when they start working.

We all know **NETWORKING** is the key to businesses and success.

☐ **Event at School? Your child has not gotten an opportunity on the stage?** Be Positive. Ask them to take opportunity backstage. Ask your child how s/he would like to describe the event to you. There are a lot of things that happen behind the stage, ask them to speak about them and check on their learnings.

☐ **Do they love to eat a specific food?** Why not ask them to research on it and encourage others to eat it too.

Do they love to wear a specific brand? Ask them to research and speak on it. They can speak about the organization (the manufacturer), it's legacy, why do they prefer it, why this brand and why not others? Have they tried another brand?

Are they health conscious? What more could be better if it comes from a child?

Is there any social issue they are concerned about?

A thorough research will help them to understand different perspectives and take a pragmatic view before they form their opinion. Impulse decision making will be to the minimal by the time they grow up. This way they would not only improve their general knowledge, understanding of the practical side of business but also skills of persuasion.

☐ **A Problem Situation?** What was the starting point of the problem that occurred and how did it get resolved. What was the learning from it?

☐Encourage Reading

Book Reading at night? Encourage them to develop their reading habit. Even if they read 2 pages at night, it is perfectly OK. Ask them to give a review of book or the 2 pages they have read verbally.

Use Sundays - Ask them to read a favourite section of theirs in the newspaper every Sunday. Ask them to speak on it in front of the entire family thereafter.

These will improve their comprehension skills. For every competitive exam, which the child will appear in the future, they would be able to ace all the sections, especially, the **READING COMPREHENSION** section very easily.

Chapter 22: The Bonus Section

Diaphragmatic Breathing Exercise
Breathing from your diaphragm expands your lungs; you noticed I didn't say "fills" your lungs. Fill your diaphragm and your

lungs will expand out to the sides and front—NOT UP toward your ears.

If you are not already a diaphragmatic, lung-expanding breather it is often easier to begin this exercise while lying down. Believe me, I could not breathe from my diaphragm standing up when I first started in acting. It was easier for me to do this lying down, then working my way to a sitting position, until I could stand up and not have to think about it.

This does take time, you have to strengthen your diaphragmatic muscle and depending on your work habits … you might get it in a few weeks or a few months. I know it took me a couple of months to get it down to the point where it became a natural habit. Yes, I still get lazy and breathe from my lungs, but the minute you stick me in front of an audience of any size, my diaphragmatic breathing kicks into gear. It's that subconscious memory, put me on a stage and I don't even have to think, "Am I breathing correctly?" It automatically happens.

Following on the next page is a quick reference to the exercise.

Notice where the diaphragm muscle is located, just below your lungs. It stretches across your upper belly area. Once you lie down, you can either use your hand or a regular hard cover-sized book and place it on your diaphragm. Personally, I believe it's easier to do this exercise with a book so your arms and hands are totally relaxed at your side; therefore I will only reference the book for the sake of this exercise.

1. Lie on your back.
2. Place the book on your diaphragm.
3. Breathe in from your nose into your diaphragm.
4. Your chest should expand out (not toward your ears).
5. As you breathe in, your diaphragm should expand toward the ceiling, making the book rise up.

6. And exhale.

7. Get that diaphragmatic muscle trained by practicing breathing slow in and out to the count of five.

Here we go:

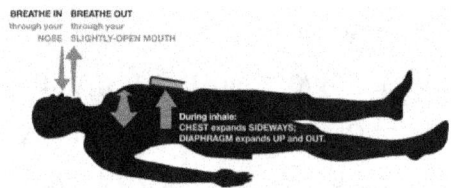

Step 1. Lie down on your back on the floor or on your bed with your book easy to reach. And for goodness sake if lying on the floor is too hard for you, DON'T DO IT, use your bed. Get comfortable, lie straight and don't cross your legs. Now place the book on your diaphragm, hands at your side.

RELAX, and breathe normally. RELAX.

Now lightly hold your lips closed, no tension, lightly. Picture in your mind a channel of air flowing into your nostrils, hooking down to your throat, through your esophagus and filling your diaphragm area. Now with your lips lightly closed, breathe in through your nostrils and feel that channel of air flowing down to your diaphragm. It's okay if this takes a few times. The book on your diaphragm should go up; your chest should expand outward. If you find your chest or your shoulders are moving toward your ears, you are not breathing correctly so try, try, try again. Get this step down before you move on.

The reason I have you breathing in through your nostrils and keeping your lips slightly closed helps you concentrate on the air flowing in and down to your diaphragm.

Step 2. Once that book is moving up and your lungs are expanding outward, take another breath in from your nose, let your diaphragm fill to the count of five (5). Now slightly separate your lips and exhale through your mouth slowly to the count of five (5).

READY???

So you'll take a breath in (one) ... two ... three ... four ... five as your diaphragm fills ... now open your lips slightly then begin to exhale (fhoooo ... two ... three ... four ... five. Good.

Step 3. Repeat this exercise twenty (20) times a day. A good time to do this is when you first wake up in the morning and when you lie down for the evening. Ten times in the morning ... ten times in the evening. Once you master breathing this way, you can take in air from both your mouth and nose.

If you think you have conquered the breathing exercise while lying down, try it now from a sitting position; if you can't do it sitting yet, go back to lying down until you have that diaphragmatic muscle so trained you can sit while breathing from your diaphragm. If you can do it sitting, you'll be standing and breathing correctly in no time. Now all that's left is to make it a speaking habit.

Keep in mind, breathing slowly in and out from your diaphragm 3-5 times before you have to speak will help relax you.

Chapter 23: Do You Have The Ability To Draw People As A Professional Speaker?

A speaker's ability to motivate is the hidden treasure in any presentation. Without it, many presentations fail no matter how good they might be. Lackluster speaking skills and unpolished scripts can still be presented well when motivation and passion shines through in the delivery! How do you measure up? 95% of your speaking engagement requires engaging an audience who may or may not want to be there and it is up to you to draw them into your presentation.

Engaging your audience requires the professional speaker to make solid connections with every single person in the room. While addressing the masses, the speaker is able to relate individually to each person and speak into their hearts and minds. A real change is made in the audience as they receive the information they have been given.

External influences impact the success of engaging your audience in your presentation. Your tone of voice should clearly communicate your passion and excitement about the topic you're speaking on. Your attire should communicate a relatable degree of professionalism. Additionally, it should also establish you as a leader or subject matter expert. Your body language should not contradict your excitement, but should exude confidence and power as you address your audience.

People are drawn in to your message when you add the personal touch to your presentation. Here are some things you can do to add the personal touch to your presentation.

1. Appeal to the emotional aspect of the problem you present. What drives someone to feel that they have to attend your speaking engagement? Address the

fear, the fulfillment of reaching dreams and goals and also the pain that comes when setbacks occur.

2. Get your audience to talk about themselves. Have them talk about their experiences. Have them share the way they feel about problems and issues they have concerning your topic.

3. Talk about real life experiences. Talk about what you or others went through in dealing with your subject (i.e. - the chaotic experiences of managing lifestyle, problems faced when dealing with implementing your solutions, etc.)

4. Make eye contact with as many audience members as possible. Your audience needs to feel like you're speaking directly to them. Eye contact is one of those subtle one-on-one connections that cannot be bypassed.

5. Be a resource for your audience. Don't be afraid to give more information than your presentation allows. Answer all questions that are asked. Ensure that the

solutions you present are simple to implement in anyone's lifestyle.

Drawing people into your presentation will ensure that you are able to connect with your audience. By making your audience a part of your presentation, they will be more attentive to what you have to say and will be more likely to take action on what you've discussed. Motivation comes as a result of making an individual connection with your audience. Not only will your information pass to your audience, but so will your passion for the topic you're speaking pass on as well. You can be a powerful speaker that gets results! Start today to practice drawing people into your presentation!

Maintaining Focus In Public Speaking

A public speaking situation can be intimidating for even the most seasoned of public speaking professionals. That is because when speaking to a live audience, you really never know what is going to happen. Never mind the freak occurrences of problems with the audience and the room, you as a human being could be subject to momentary memory halts that often come as the result of nervousness or just looking up and seeing all those eyes looking at you.

So much of the discipline of giving a public presentation is to establish an internal structure to your talk that helps you stay on task and maintain the focus of your subject for the entire time you are speaking. That structure can also be of huge value in helping you gauge your time and make adjustments so you get the most crucial parts of your talk presented within the allocated time frame even if that means leaving out less important parts of your presentation.

There is a simple directive many public speakers live by that gives you a fine guideline for that structure. It goes like this...

. Tell them what you are going to do. . Do what you said you were going to do . Tell them you did it.

This simple outline may be overly simplistic but it is the heart of what makes a good presentation work. And the simplicity also helps you stay focused under the pressure of a public speaking situation. So any tool that can do that is a good one.

You tell the audience what to expect during your opening comments. Those comments also contact giving your personal information, a greeting to the audience and perhaps some humor to set the tone of the talk. After you have gotten the speech underway, it is common to establish what is the topic of your talk. But to do that, the most effective device is to make a statement of the problem. By phrasing the subject matter as a compelling and very real problem to your audience, that creates interest as the audience says mentally, "Yes I have that problem. Tell me how you will help me fix it."

This is where you tell them what you are going to do. The body of your speech is usually a three to five point discussion of the solution to the problem. Don't give them the entire heart of your speech but let them know the ground you are about to cover. Not only does this give the audience a road map of what to expect, it lets them know that you know what you are doing and you know when you will get done. This gets rid of a secret fear of an out of control speaker that a lot of people who sit in on presentations dread.

Once you establish this roadmap for the rest of your speech, this gives the audience a good feel for where you will be going. By giving them this information early on, that actually reduces the impulse to interrupt you because they know you have a path to go on and they don't want to take you off that path. Now it is just a matter of stepping through each of the outlined areas to do for this audience what you said you would do which is to offer a solution to the problem statement. Naturally your detailed discussion will have more content than your brief preview. But if you continue to broadcast to the audience where you are on the outline and that you are on track to reach the goal, that keeps them interested and assured that this is an organized program they are a part of.

It is always good to let the audience know then when you are entering your closing statements. Many speakers use a simple clue like "Let me point out, and I am closing with this..." to give the audience the signal that the presentation is almost done. This is common courtesy and a professional way to conduct a presentation. And if you treat the audience with respect like this by telling them what you are going to do, do it and then tell them you did it, you will be a speaker that will get good reviews and invited back for more presentations frequently.

Make Them Laugh

In the delightful Broadway musical "Singing in the Rain", there is a song called "Make em Laugh" which is based on this idea that the best way for any stage performer to build a bond with an audience is to use humor to bring a smile, or a laugh, to that audience. Well, that idea is not just valid for stage performers. It's just as true when you begin to develop your style as a public speaker.

If you pick up any self help guide to how to be effective as a public speaker, one of the golden rules is to open with a joke. But guess what? That is not actually a hard and fast rule. Humor is the type of thing that works just as well about a minute into your presentation, halfway through or just about anywhere that you feel you are losing your audience.

Audience psychology is a funny thing but not in the "laughter" sense. The truth is that when you first begin to speak to an audience, they are probably listening to you. Most people are at least curious about you and what you have to say and will take interest in you if for no other reason than you are a new person up there in front of them. While there is certainly not a bad idea to open with humor, the time your audience needs a joke is when you have launched into your discussion and you look out to nodding heads or drifting eyes and you know that you are talking but nobody is listening. That is when humor brings the audience back to you and hooks them back into your presentation.

The biggest problem with a lot of public speaking situations is that you may be presenting ideas to the crowd. While an idea is a good thing, people have trouble staying focused on pure concepts for very long. That is why most good public speakers use illustrations, stories and humor to keep the audience focused on what you are talking about. And that is where a generous use of humor will help your public speaking style as well.

Humor has a certain effect on the human psychology that causes the listener to bond with the speaker in a unique way. To put that more simply, using humor in your presentation makes people like you. And when they like you, they want to hear what you have to say. There is just no getting around the fact that people will listen to, accept, understand and make their own ideas presented with humor far more readily than if your talk is dry presentation of material, even if it is important material.

But what if you don't know how to use humor? Of course you can always just tell a joke. But canned jokes are just that, attempts to use someone else's humor. They do work, (if it's a good joke) but if the humor is not relevant to what you are talking about or to you as a speaker, it often is not as effective as it should be.

The best humor is actually self-deprecating remarks as you speak. These are easy to come up with by simply using yourself as the subject of an illustration. For example, if this topic was part of your speech, you might say...

"You know it's easy to get tongue tied and bumble around up here trying to use humor. But you folks won't make a mess of it like I am doing."

That isn't even a very good joke. But because it is highly relevant, it is self deprecating and it's a light moment in the presentation, it will probably get a chuckle. A chuckle is really all you are looking for. You are not trying to become a stand up comic up there. Humor that is too wild and designed to bring hearty laughter actually is distracting. You just want little asides that are of a humorous nature to bring your audience back to listening to you.

Listen to good speakers you admire and take note of how they seem to slip and out of humor easily and effortlessly and how quickly that build rapport with the audience. It will take some practice to get good at using humor as you speak. But it will improve your presentation style tremendously. And that's the whole idea, isn't it?

Chapter 24: Factors That Cause Public Speaking Anxiousness

Even the most experienced speaker gets anxious when speaking in public. Nonetheless, this fear could be managed so that you could put your fear to your advantage. This topic teaches us why people are nervous when speaking in front of a crowd and how you could conquer your fear.

Fear of the audience

People are scared of rejection by their audience. Thus, many are terrified of speaking in public for fear of being criticized by the crowd for how they look or how they deliver their speech. On the contrary, audiences are quite comprehending about the speaker's problem with stage fright. You become more nervous when your fear of the audience raises.

Beneath are a few strategies that could help you overcome your fear of the audience.

\> Select a topic that you like and you are familiar with. The more comfy you are about your selected topic, the more confident you are in facing your audience.

\> Focus on your topic. Concentrate on your topic and not on your self. Whenever you start to think of your subject matter and not your self, your fear of speaking will likely decrease.

\> Say to your self: "I am the Chief." Trust in your capacity of delivering your speech. Showing that you are in charge reduces your fear and raises your self-confidence in facing the scenario.

\> Don't think of your audience as a threat. Bridge the gap between your audience and your self. Analyze cautiously to establish rapport. You ought to consider age, gender and their level of expertise. Recall to analyze your audience.

Fear of failure

Phere are two ways to win over your fear of failure.

> Picture your self succeeding. If you think that you will stutter in front of many individuals, chances are you will stutter. But if you picture your self delivering your speech well, then, you will.

> Face your fear. You can not overcome your fear unless you show it and admit that you are worried of it. Fear that your speech is a bad speech

> Write well. Take time to write your speech. Review it and rewrite if necessary. If you are confident with your speech, the less terrified you will be about speaking in public.

> Practice and ask for suggestions on how you could improve your speech. Ask a friend of relative to act as your audience. Once you have delivered your topic, ask for their feedback. Don't be frightened to hear about what they will say. Their feedback could give you insight on what's good or bad in your speech.

Chapter 25: Humor

Why should you bother using humor in your public speaking career? Using humor in your presentation has great value. It serves several purposes. As we all know, there is a little nervousness in both the presenter and the audience. Appropriate humor relaxes an audience and makes it feel more comfortable with you as the presenter. Humor can bring attention to the point you are making and will help the audience better remember your point.

Humor can break down barriers so the audience is more receptive to your ideas. When you use humor in a public setting especially when you are speaking to a business audience or any audience who is not specifically there for humor, make the humor reinforce your point and you will get a much better response.

It is a good idea to open your presentation with some sort of humor. This is called a "ho-humcrasher". This will set the audience and yourself at ease and help relax all, including you. When opening your presentation with humor, listen to their reaction and gauge their reaction to see if it is necessary to adjust your delivery.

The best and easiest place to find humor

for your presentation is from your own personal experiences. Presenting safe humor is very important. Remember, using humor outside of "you" has the possibility of back-firing. Caution is requested here. Using yourself as the point of the humor is the safest. Think back on an embarrassing moment that you, at the time, thought was not funny. But thinking back on it now, it really was funny and you can laugh about it now. This type of humor is great to share with your audience. **I call it the "Stoop Factor"; defined simply, it is something I did that was really stupid**. This is normally safe humor because you are making fun of yourself.

Make sure the humor is funny to you. If you don't laugh or smile at the humor, then you certainly cannot expect an audience to do so. A key to using humor is only using humor that makes you laugh or smile. **"I use humor throughout my presentations because I love what I do**

and always have fun when presenting. Heck and I get paid for it too!"

Before using humor in your presentation, try it out with small groups. Did they laugh and enjoy it? Even if your group did not laugh or smile initially, don't give up on humor, because the problem might be in the way it was delivered. Keep practicing and you will get there. **There is nothing worse than listening to a monotone, non-entertaining speaker. Get it on! Show some fire and humor out there!**

Make sure the humor relates to the point you are making. Do not use humor that is simply there to make the audience laugh. The comedy shop is full of comedians. The humor should tie in with some portion of your presentation so as the audience enjoys the humor, but, also remembers the point being made.

When possible, choose humor that comes from people you interact with. You do not have to worry about people having heard it before, and you will feel more comfortable with what has happened to you. Find such experiences by looking for a humorous line or situation.

We have discussed a lot about the value of humor, but how is it delivered? There are several ways to accomplish this. One thing to learn is how to deliver a punch line and when. Let's look at the "punch line". A punch line is the final part of a joke, usually the word, sentence or exchange of sentences which is intended to be funny and to provoke laughter from listeners. Delivery is not a hard technique to learn. Your punch line is delivered a little harder and with a slightly different voice than the rest of the joke. You may want to lean into the microphone and state the punch line louder and more clearly than you said the setup lines. If the audience does not hear the punch line, they are not going to laugh. Just before the punch line you should pause slightly to emphasize and draw special attention to the line.

After you deliver the line, don't make a sound. Give the audience a chance to laugh. This will be hard for you to do as you will be tempted to add more to the punch line if there is no immediate response. **The key here is just shut-up and wait!** Until you get more experience, waiting will be a challenge. New public speakers tend to fear that no laughter will come, so they keep talking. If you keep talking during this period, you will easily kill the laughter. As your success in this area grows, confidence builds and pausing will become. Sometimes waiting the audience out will actually give them a sign to laugh even if the joke wasn't that good. We have the punch line thing addressed and how to deliver it. But who do we deliver it to?

When you deliver your punch line, deliver it to one person only. It doesn't matter how large the audience is, you can look one person right in the eye and deliver the line. Don't just pick a person at random.

Doing this can cause a problem. In Chapter 10 "Event Day" we talk about meeting attendees during a planned social hour or meeting attendees before the presentation. Meeting the participants and finding out who would be fun and receptive to your humor is important. Find out where they are sitting. That way you can look directly at them during the presentation. **General rule is "deliver your punch lines to a person you know is going to laugh."** Pay attention and know your audience. Observe the audience every chance you get prior to your presentation. There will be opportunities during the program prior to you presenting, maybe while the program coordinator or M/C is talking or another speaker. **Basically, know the dance floor before you get up and dance!**

Conclusion

Well here we are. As I have mentioned before, there are many public speakers out in the world but how many of them are effective hence successful public speakers, is another matter. Think of success in public speaking and all that this could mean for you: that sense of personal accomplishment; that boost in your self-esteem and self-confidence; that boost in your efforts at advocacy (regarding some cause close to your heart); that boost in your career.

I know that during my many years as a Communications Manager, when looking for new talent to join my team, I placed public speaking skills at the top of my list. In general, organizations also tend to be on a constant lookout for speakers who could effectively articulate organizational brands, objectives and outcomes.

So the possibilities are endless. But, your sense of confidence and empowerment from developing and honing your public speaking skills doesn't stop there. It will often spread to other areas of your lives.

I hope that all that I have shared with you in this book will serve you well in your public speaking efforts. With these **public speaking made simple** steps at your fingertips, don't you think it is time for you to **embrace the process?**

Go forth and triumph.

www.ingramcontent.com/pod-product-compliance
Lightning Source LLC
Chambersburg PA
CBHW072003070526
44583CB00015B/1308